Rich Dad's

Guide to

Raising Your Child's Financial I.Q.

Published by
TechPress, Inc.
6611 N. 64th Place
Paradise Valley, Arizona 85253 U.S.A.
602-998-6971

"CASHFLOW" is the registered trademark of
CASHFLOW Technologies, Inc.

E B   E|B   E|B   E|B   are trademarks of
S I   S|I   S|I   S|I
CASHFLOW Technologies, Inc.

CASHFLOW for KIDS is the trademark of
CASHFLOW Technologies, Inc.

Kiyosaki, Robert T. and Lechter, Sharon L.
Rich Dad's Guide to: Raising your Child's Financial
I.Q./Robert T. Kiyosaki with Sharon L. Lechter and
Ann Nevin Pd.D.
p. cm.
ISBN 0-9643856-4-3 Pbk.
1. Personal Finance 2. Business Education
3. Success - Financial 4. Investments 5. Parenting
I. Title

Designed by Insync Graphic Studio, Inc.
Printed in the China.
RDRCIQ.CTI.IGS.SKP/799-987654321

From an Expert

As a mathematics professor in the College of Education at Arizona State University West and as the principal investigator for a 2 million dollar grant from the National Science Foundation to promote mathematics learning in the primary grades, I send this letter in support of the game CASHFLOW for KIDS.

This game was beneficial for my children because I could immediately see an improvement in their mathematics knowledge and their understanding of money. The game is self rewarding and my children (brothers) wanted to play it again after they finished playing the very first time. In their second game they made their decisions faster and their decisions were more strategically planned than in the first round.

As a parent, I was pleased to observe the money attitudes of my children as they played the game. They learned from the choices they made accelerating their understanding in future games. CASHFLOW for KIDS is a great learning tool for all children.

I thank you for a game that simplifies the complex subjects of mathematics and money so that all children can participate in the game and grow in knowledge as they play.

Yolanda De La Cruz, Ph.D.
Ph.D. University of California at Berkeley
Professor of Mathematics,
College of Education,
Arizona State University West

Dedicated to Parents and Teachers Everywhere

CASHFLOW for KIDS was designed to help you, as a parent or teacher, give your child a financial head start in life. Our children will be required to learn much more than we ever did, and much more than schools are prepared to teach them. Financial Education is essential to ensure our children have secure and happy futures.

Remember our Children are our Future!

Table of Contents

INTRODUCTION

Who Teaches Your Children?

My rich dad often said, "If you don't teach your children about money, there are many people who will." Today we are educated financially from many sources. Sources that often have something to sell you. On television, you see sports stars selling a particular brand of shoe. Or another celebrity saying, "Clean up your high interest credit card debt with a bill consolidation loan using the equity in your home." The star then winks and says, "And you're smart for doing this because you get a tax break from the government for being in debt longer." In other words, take short-term high interest credit card debt and convert it into lower interest long-term debt. Then your banker tells you your house is an asset, but doesn't tell you whose asset it really is. Today even airlines are in the credit business. They encourage you to use their credit cards so you can receive miles for free trips. Retailers entice you by saying, "Low down easy monthly payments." And financial institutions beam out at you, "Save money, and invest for the long term." Even our educational system is in the fray. Today, many young people leave school deeply in debt owing tens of thousands of dollars for their college education. In the Information Age this is how we are being financially educated but it is not the right type of financial education.

Financial Education is Taught at Home

My book, **Rich Dad Poor Dad**, is a true story based upon my two fathers, one rich and one poor. One educated and the other never finished school. One was a highly paid government employee and the other a very wealthy business owner and investor. One dad was my real father and my other dad was my best friend's father. Both men were strong, dynamic, successful men. Both were very honest hard working men, but when it came to the subject of money, both men had very different ideas. After reading the book, many people think **Rich Dad Poor Dad** is a book about money. It really isn't. It is really a book about education.

My highly educated but poor dad sincerely believed that what you learned in school was most important to a successful life. He believed that a good academic education was all you needed to ensure job security and a life of success. On the other hand my rich dad, who dropped out of school to take over the family business when his father died, believed that what you learned outside of school was just as important. He agreed that what you learned in school was important, but not that it would ensure a life of financial success. For this reason he took an active interest in educating his son and me about money. He spent hours, days, and even years, teaching us what he thought was important for us to learn. Subjects not taught in school, but essential for all of us to learn...especially today.

In earlier times, a child's education was left entirely up to the parents. During the era of hunter-gatherers, the father taught the son to hunt as well as to protect the tribe. The mother taught the daughter to tend to chores in the camp, tan hides, and raise the children. Both parents taught their children the social values of the tribe, respect of elders, how to handle disputes amongst people of the tribe, as well as songs, customs, stories, and rituals that bound the tribe together and made them whole. During the Agrarian Age, mother and father still worked as a team, not only managing the farm or family business, but also in raising the children. In the Agrarian Age, both parents still had close personal contact with their children.

Then came the Industrial Age or what I call the "Leave it to Beaver" era. During this period, the father left home to work and to bring home the paycheck. The mother stayed at home to make a comfortable nest for the family and the children went off to school. In other words, the state became responsible for teaching the children what it thought was important. During this period, there was still a lot of family time, but that family time was becoming more scarce.

Today, we are in the Information Age and now often both parents work, just to make ends meet. The kids often come home to an empty house, turn on the TV, play organized sports under a parent-coach, spend hours at the mall, play video games by the hour, or spend hours on the phone or the internet.

Instead of having their parents as teachers, today's children are subjected to literally millions of teachers, in person and electronically. This is a major reason parents have less control over their children today.

We All Need Financial Education

The April 18, 1999, Sunday issue of Parade Magazine in the U.S. ran a cover headline that said,

"What We Don't Know About Money Will Hurt Us."

The National Council on Economic Education tested 1010 adults and 1085 high school students on their knowledge of basic economic principles. The results were:

Among Adults	**Among High School Students**
• 6% got an A	• 3% got an A
• 10% got a B	• 7% got a B
• 15% got a C	• 11% got a C
• 20% got a D	• 13% got a D
• 49% got an F	• 66% got an F

In other words 69% of all adults scored below a C and 79% of all students scored below a C. The shocking part about the article was the simplicity of the questions that were failed. Simple questions about inflation and supply and demand cycles.

Another startling fact was that while 38 states offer courses in economics, only 13 states required the students to take an economics course to graduate.

Personal finance was given even less importance in most schools, a subject I think that is even more important than economics. Only two states, New York and Illinois, required that a course in personal finance be taken for graduation.

The encouraging news is that attitudes in the educational system are beginning to change. The fact that these articles were written shows that there is now awareness for the need of financial education. However the question remains, will the change be in time and will the information taught be adequate to handle the realities of life?

The Information Age is Different

In feudal times, only the monarch and his or her friends could be rich. The Industrial Age made great wealth available to many more people and their friends. In the Information Age, the possibility of great wealth for the masses has been greatly expanded. Today, not only can you attain great wealth you can attain it faster. Just look at Bill Gates, founder of Microsoft as an example. While in his thirties, he became the richest man in the world. Today, we have twenty-year-old self-made billionaires…young people born in the 1970's and 1980's. At the same time we have baby-boomers still dreaming about a $50,000 a year job. Many of these boomers are struggling financially because they are still following their parent's advice of "Get a safe, secure job," not realizing that times have changed.

Historians have noted that great changes have occurred every 500 years. In 1492, Christopher Columbus sailed the ocean blue. It is also believed that his voyage marked the beginning of the Industrial Age. In 1989, the Berlin Wall came down. There are a few economic historians who say that that event marked the end of the Industrial Age and the beginning of the Information Age. Unfortunately, there are millions of people who are still operating by the rules of the Industrial Age. Millions of people still passing on Industrial Age advice to their children, the same advice their parents gave them.

Like it or not, we seem to be living at the end of one of those 500 year eras. As we pass the year 2000, there will be more and more accelerating change. Millions of people will find life financially tougher. While still others will find wealth beyond the wealth of kings and queens of old. One great thing about the Information age is that we all have more access to information.

This book and educational game, CASHFLOW for KIDS, were created to give parents and teachers tools via which to teach children valuable financial life skills while having fun and spending more time with their children. This book and educational game are about preparing children for the future, for ultimately, they are the future.

NOTE: A lot of the information in this book has also been presented in my other books in the Rich Dad series. I felt it was important to provide you with the basics of what is taught through all of our products, so you can better understand the overall program and therefore be better prepared to teach your children. If you have read the other books, some of the information in this book will be redundant. If you have not read the other books, and have further questions about the material presented in this book, you may find more in depth explanations in our other books and products.

Added Educational Viewpoints

To increase the educational value of this book, we are including the professional comments from Dr. Ann Nevin, a leading authority on educating children, as well as Sharon Lechter, a CPA and a mom. Their comments will appear at the end of each chapter to give a more complete explanation and review of some of my rich dad's ideas on money.

Robert Kiyosaki

A Note From Ann Nevin Ph.D.

As an educational psychologist with over 3 decades of experience in teaching, and researching methods of effective teaching and learning, I have become increasingly alarmed at the failure of our public schools. I share Robert Kiyosaki's concerns about the new demands that the Information Age places on all of us, especially our children. Because schools cannot teach our children everything, it becomes even more important for the family and community to be aware of meaningful and beneficial methods that encourage our children to learn.

The ideas presented in this book and the game, CASHFLOW for KIDS, are based on tried and true principles of learning that have been shown to accelerate and stimulate children's learning.

Throughout history, games have been used as powerful teaching tools. Royalty of old used games such as Chess and Backgammon to teach leadership and military strategy to their children. Another thing I like about this game being a board game, rather than an electronic game, is that it requires interaction with other human beings. Too often today our children study alone, sit in front of a computer screen alone, and watch TV alone. A vital part of learning is to learn to be involved, giving, taking, and sharing with a real person. CASHFLOW fir KIDS being a board game teaches not only vital financial skills but also vital human interaction skills.

Games have another added benefit. Games often reflect back a person's true behavior. For example, if a person is too conservative or too risk adverse, that behavior will show up in the game. If a person is prone to taking excessive risk, that behavior will also show up. If a person is one who breaks the rules or is prone to cheat, that core behavior will also show up. So while playing CASHFLOW for KIDS, a parent could be advised to observe a child's behavior, commenting on the behavior not the child, as the game is in process. In other words, you can learn a lot about yourself and others from a simple little game.

A Note Form Sharon Lechter, CPA

CASHFLOW for KIDS was designed to help you, as a parent or teacher, give your children a financial head start in life. Our children will be required to learn much more than we ever did, and much more than schools are prepared to teach them. Cash flow management is an essential life skill and a skill that will require much more sophistication as we move further into the Information Age. CASHFLOW for KIDS was developed:

1. To give children an understanding of the subject of money.
2. To teach children the life skill of personal cash flow management.
3. To inspire an interest in the subject of money and further personal study of the subject.
4. To teach this information in a fun way.
5. To help the parent or teacher discover how each child best learns.
6. To bring the parent or teacher and child closer through playing and learning together.
7. To introduce children to the basics of financial literacy.
8. To teach often complex accounting terms as simply as possible.

CHAPTER 1

Does Your Child Have A High Financial I.Q.?

When you say someone has a high IQ, what does that mean? What does your IQ measure? Does having a high IQ guarantee that you will be successful? Does having a high IQ mean you will be rich?

When I was in the fourth grade, my teacher announced to the class, "Students, we are honored to have a genius in our midst. He is a very gifted child and he has a very high IQ." She then went on to announce that one of my best friends, Andrew, was one of the brightest students she had ever had the privilege to teach. Up until that time, "Andy the Ant" as we all called Andrew was just one of the kids in the class. We called him "Andy the Ant" because he was tiny and had thick glasses that made him look like a bug. Now we had to call him "Andy the Brainy Ant."

Not understanding what "IQ" meant I raised my hand and asked the teacher, "What does IQ mean?"

The teacher sputtered a little and replied, "IQ means Intelligence Quotient." She then gave me one of those looks that said silently, "Now do you know what IQ means?" as she glared down her nose.

The problem was, I still had no idea what "IQ" meant so I raised my hand again. The teacher did her best to ignore me, but finally she turned and said in a long drawn out tone, "Yes. What is your question this time?"

"Well you said 'IQ' stood for Intelligence Quotient, but what does that mean?"

Again she sputtered a little with impatience. "I told you that if you did not know the definition of something that you should look it up. Now get the dictionary and look it up for yourself."

"OK," I said with a grin, realizing that she did not know the definition either. If she had known, she would have proudly told the entire class. We knew that when she did not know something, she would never admit it but instead tell us to look it up.

Finally locating "Intelligence Quotient" in the dictionary, I read the definition out loud. Quoting directly I read, "Noun (1916) A number used to express the apparent relative intelligence of a person determined by dividing his mental age as reported on a standardized test by his chronological age and multiplying by 100." After reading the definition, I looked up and said, "I still don't understand what IQ means."

Frustrated, the teacher raised her voice and said, "You don't understand because you don't want to understand. If you don't understand it, then you need to do your own research."

"But you're the one who said it was important," I shot back. "If you think it's important, at least you can tell us what it means and why it's important."

At that point, Andy the Ant stood up and said, "I'll explain it to the class." Climbing out from behind his wooden desk he walked to the chalkboard at the front of the room. He then wrote on the board,

$$\frac{18 \ (\text{mental age})}{10 \ (\text{chronological age})} \ X \ 100 = 180 \ IQ$$

"So people say I am a genius because I am 10 years of age but have test scores of a person who is 18 years of age."

The class sat silently for awhile to digest the information that Andy had just put on the board.

"In other words, if you don't increase your abilities to learn as you get older, then your IQ could come down," I said.

"That's how I would interpret it," said Andy. "I might be a genius today but if I don't increase what I know, my IQ comes down with each year. At least that is what the equation represents."

"So you could be a genius today but be a dummy tomorrow," I said with a laugh.

"Very funny," said Andy. "But accurate. Yet I know I don't have to worry about you beating me."

"I'll get even after school," I shouted back. "I'll meet you on the baseball diamond and then we'll see who has the higher IQ." With that I laughed and so did other students in the class. Andy the Ant was one of my best friends. We all knew he was smart and we knew he would never be a great athlete. Yet even though he could not hit or catch the ball, he was still very much a part of our team. After all, that is what friends are for.

What Is Your Financial IQ?

So how do you measure people's Financial IQ? Do you measure it by how big their paycheck is, by their net worth, the kind of car they drive, or by the size of their house?

Several years later, long after the discussion about Andy the Ant being a genius, I asked my rich dad what he thought Financial IQ meant. He quickly stated "Financial intelligence is not about how much money you make, but how much money you keep, and how hard that money works for you."

Yet as time went on, he refined his definition of financial intelligence. He once said, "You know your financial intelligence is increasing if as you get older your money is buying you more freedom, happiness, health, and choices in life." He went on to explain, that many people made more money as they got older, but their money only bought them less freedom. Less freedom in the form of having bigger bills to pay. Having bigger bills meant the person had to work harder to pay them. To rich dad this was not financially intelligent. He also explained that he saw many people making a lot of money but their money did not make them happier. To him, that was not financially intelligent. "Why work for money and be unhappy?" He said. "If you must work for money find a way to work and be happy. That is financial intelligence."

When it came to health he would say, "Too many people work too hard for money and slowly kill themselves in the process. Why work hard sacrificing the mental and physical well-being of your family as well as yourself? That is not financially intelligent." When it came to health he also said, "There is no such thing as a sudden heart attack. Heart attacks and other diseases such as cancer take time to develop. They are caused by lack of exercise, a poor diet, and not enough joy in one's life over extended periods of time. Of the three, I think the lack of joy is the greatest cause of heart attacks and disease." He said, "Too many people think about working harder rather than think about how to have more fun and enjoy this great gift of life."

And when it came to choices he would say this, "I know the first class section of an airplane arrives at the same time as the economy section. That is not the issue. The issue is, do you have the choice of flying first class or flying economy? Most people in the economy section have no choice." My rich dad went on to explain that financial intelligence gave a person more choices in life by saying, "Money is power because more money gives you more choices". But it was his lesson about happiness that he stressed more and more the older he got. As he neared the end of his life and he had more money than he had dreamed possible, he restated again and again, "Money does not make you happy. Never think that you will be happy when you get rich. If you are not happy while getting rich, chances are you will not be happy when you do get rich. So regardless if you are rich or poor, make sure you are happy."

For those of you who have read my other books, you realize that my rich dad did not measure his Financial IQ in traditional financial measurements. In other words, he was never really fixated by how much money he had, or his net worth, or the size of his portfolio. If I were to define what financial intelligence bought him, it would be "freedom."

He loved having the freedom to work or to not work. The freedom to choose with whom he worked. He loved the freedom to buy whatever he wanted without worrying about the price. He loved the health, happiness, and choices he could afford because he was free. He loved the freedom and financial ability he had to donate to charity to help causes he believed in. And instead of complaining about politicians and feeling powerless to change the system, he had politicians coming to him seeking his advice (and hoping for his campaign contributions). He loved having power over them. "They call me, I don't call them.

Every politician wants the poor person's vote, but they don't listen to the poor person. They really can't afford to…and that is tragic." He said.

Yet, what he cherished most was the free time that money bought him. He loved having the time to watch his children grow up and to work on projects that interested him, whether or not they made money. So my rich dad measured his Financial IQ in time, more than money. The last few years of his life were the most joyous because he spent most of his time giving his money away, rather than trying to conserve and hang onto it. He seemed to have as much fun giving it away as a philanthropist as he did making it as a capitalist. He lived a rich, happy, and generous life. Most importantly, he had a life of boundless freedom and that is how he measured his Financial IQ.

What is Intelligence?

It was my real dad, the head of education and gifted teacher that ultimately became the personal tutor to "Andy the Ant." Andy was so smart that he should have been in his senior year of high school rather than the fifth grade. His mom and dad were pressured to have him skip many grades, yet they wanted him to stay with his age group. Since my real dad was also an academic genius, a person who graduated from a four-year university in two years, he understood what Andy was going through and respected his parent's wishes. In many ways he agreed with them, realizing that academic age is not as important as emotional and physical development. He agreed that Andy should mature emotionally and physically, rather than go to high school or college with students twice his age. So after attending elementary school with regular kids, "Andy the Ant" would go to my dad, the Superintendent of Education, and spend the afternoons studying with him. I, on the other hand, went to my rich dad's office and began my education in financial intelligence.

I find it interesting to reflect back upon the fact that different fathers took it upon themselves to spend time teaching other parent's children. It's nice to see it still happening today as many parents volunteer their time to teach sports, arts, music, dance, crafts, business skills and more. Ultimately, all adults are teachers in one way or another...and as adults we are teachers more by our actions than by our words.

When our teacher announced to the class that Andy the Ant was a genius with a high IQ, in essence she also told us that the rest of us were not. I went home and asked my dad what his definition of intelligence was. His reply was simple. All he said was, "Intelligence is the ability to make finer distinctions."

I stood there for a moment not understanding what he had said. So I waited for him to explain further, knowing that because he was a true teacher, he could not leave me standing there with a dumb expression on my face. Finally, he realized that I did not understand his explanation so he began to speak in the language of a 10 year old.

"Do you know what the word 'sports' means?" My dad asked.

"Sure I do," I said. "I love sports."

"Good," he replied. "Is there a difference between football, golf, and surfing?"

"Of course there is." I said excitedly. "There are huge differences between those sports."

"Good," my father continued in his teacher mode. "Those differences are called 'distinctions'."

"You mean distinctions are the same as differences?" I asked.

My dad nodded his head.

"So the more I can tell the differences between something, then the more intelligent I am?" I asked.

"That is correct," my dad answered. "So you have a much higher Sports IQ than Andy...but Andy has a much higher Academic IQ than you. What this really means is that Andy learns best by reading and you learn best by doing. So Andy has an easier time learning in the classroom and you have an easier time learning on the athletic field. Andy will learn history and science quickly and you will learn baseball and football quickly.

I stood there silently for awhile. My dad, being a good teacher, let me stand there until the distinctions settled in. Finally, I recovered from my trance and said, "So I learn by playing games and Andy learns by reading."

My dad nodded his head. He paused awhile and then said, "Our school system puts great importance upon Academic or Scholastic Intelligence. So when they say someone has a high IQ, they mean a high scholastic or academic IQ. The current IQ test measures primarily a person's verbal IQ. Their ability to read and write. So technically, a person with a high IQ is someone who learns quickly by reading. It does not measure all of a person's intelligence. So that IQ is not a measure of a person's artistic IQ, physical IQ, or even their mathematical intelligence, which are all legitimate intelligence's."

Continuing on I said, "So when my teacher says that Andy is a genius it means that he is better at learning by reading than I am. And I am better at learning by doing."

My dad nodded his head.

Again I stood there thinking for a moment. Slowly I began to understand how this new bit of information applied to me. "So I need to find ways to learn things that best suits my learning style." I finally said.

Again my dad nodded his head. "You still need to learn to read, but it seems that you will learn faster by doing than reading. In many ways, Andy has a problem in that he can read but cannot do. In some ways, he may find the real world a harder place to adapt to than you will. He will do well as long as he remains in the world of academics or science. And that is why he has a hard time on the baseball field or in talking to the rest of the kids. This is why I think it's great that the rest of you allow him to be on your sports teams. You are teaching him things that a schoolbook could never teach him…subjects and skills that are very important for success in the real world."

"Andy is a great friend," I said. "But he would rather read than play baseball. And I would rather play baseball than read. So it means he is smarter in the classroom because he learns better there. But that does not mean he is smarter than me. His high IQ means he is a genius at learning by reading. So I need to find a way to make more distinctions faster so I can learn faster…in a way that works best for me."

Multiply by Dividing

My educator dad smiled. "That's the attitude. Find a way to make distinctions quickly and you will learn quickly. Always remember that nature multiplies by dividing," he said. "Just as a cell increases by splitting…the same is true with intelligence. The moment we split a subject into two, we have increased our intelligence. If we then split the two into two, we get four and our intelligence is now multiplying…multiplying by dividing. That is called quantum learning not linear learning."

I nodded my head understanding how learning could get faster once I first figured out how I learned best. "When I first started playing baseball, I didn't know much." I said. "But I soon found out the difference between striking out, a home run, and a RBI. Is that what you mean by my intelligence increases by dividing or making finer distinctions?"

"That is correct," my dad replied. "And the more you play the game, the more you will keep discovering new and finer distinctions. Don't you find yourself improving as you learn more?"

"Yeah," I said. "When I first started playing

baseball, I couldn't even hit the ball. Now I can bunt, drag hit, ground the ball, or go for the fence with a home run. You know that I've hit 3 home runs this year?" I said proudly with a grin.

"Yes I know," my dad said. "And I'm very proud of you. And do you realize that there are many people who do not know the difference between a bunt and a home run? They have no idea what you're talking about and they certainly aren't able to do what you're talking about?"

"So my baseball IQ is really high," I said with a smile.

"Very high," said my dad. "Just as Andy's academic IQ is really high…but he can't hit a baseball."

"You're telling me," I said. "Andy may know the difference between a bunt and a home run, but he couldn't do either one of them if his life depended upon it."

"And that is the problem with judging a person only on their academic IQ." My educator dad said. "Often people with high IQ's do not do well in the real world."

"Why is that?" I asked.

"That is a good question that I really have no answer for. I think it is because educators focus primarily on mental skills and not on converting mental knowledge into physical knowledge. I also think that we educators punish people for making mistakes and if you are afraid of making mistakes, you will not want to do anything. We in education place too much emphasis on the need to be right and the fear of being wrong. It is the fear of making a mistake and then looking foolish that prevents people from taking action…and ultimately, we all learn via taking action. We all know we learn by making mistakes yet in our school system we punish people for making too many of them. The world of education is filled with people who can tell you all you need to know about the game of baseball, but they cannot play baseball themselves."

"So when our teacher says Andy is a genius, does that mean he's better than me?" I asked.

"No," said my dad. "But in school, he'll have an easier time learning than you will because his reading skills are at a genius level. However on the athletic field, you'll learn faster than he does. That is all it means."

"So having a high IQ may only mean he learns faster by reading…but it doesn't mean I can't learn as much as he knows." I replied seeking greater clarity. "In other words, I can learn something if I want to learn it. Isn't that true?"

"That's it," said my dad. "Education is attitude…and if you have that kind of positive attitude towards learning you will do well. But if you have a losers attitude, or a defeated attitude towards learning, then you will never learn anything."

I pulled my baseball magazine out of my back pocket. It was worn and tattered. "I love to read this magazine. I can tell you the scores, batting averages, and salaries of all the players. But when I read this magazine in classroom, my teacher takes the magazine away."

"As she should." My dad said. "But she should have encouraged you to read it after school."

I nodded my head. I finally understood why Andy had a higher IQ. But most importantly, I learned how I learned best. That day, I learned that I learn best by doing first and then reading about it. For example with baseball, the more I played the game, the more I wanted to read about it. But if I did not play the game, I had no interest in reading about it. It was a way of learning that worked best for me. It was a way I would learn for the rest of my life. If I tried something first and then found it interesting, I would be more excited about reading about it. But if I could not physically be involved first, or had to only read about something, I was rarely interested and hence did not want to read about it. Being only 10 years old, I had learned enough for the day. My attention span had been exhausted. Grabbing my baseball glove and bat I headed out the door to go make finer distinctions about the game of baseball. I had some baseball IQ to improve and practice was the best way for me to do that. Besides I knew that if I didn't keep practicing, Andy the Ant might replace me on the team.

That one explanation from my educator dad was the primary reason I finished high school and went on to survive a very tough federal military academy with a rigorous academic curriculum. Because of this explanation I knew that although I did not have a high academic IQ, it did not mean that I was not smart. It merely meant I had to find a way of learning that worked best for me. Without this valuable knowledge, I might have dropped out of school long before graduating from high school. Personally I found school too slow, too boring, and uninteresting. I was not interested in most of the subjects I was required to study, but I found a way to learn those subjects and pass the tests. What kept me going was the knowledge that once I left school with my college degree my real education would begin.

This Book is About Raising Your Child's Financial IQ

This book and the game CASHFLOW for KIDS, were created to assist parents in supplementing their child's financial education. These educational tools cannot teach a child everything he or she needs to learn…but they can help provide a strong foundation for further learning. The reason this book is a vital part of the game is because there are many things that the game cannot teach. This book was written to assist the parent and teacher in supplementing the financial lessons taught by the game. By utilizing a game, the child involves most learning modalities, which are visual, auditory, and touch. Games give all children a chance to be geniuses because games involve more than one form of IQ.

The book serves as a guide for parents to supplement the lessons designed into the game. The more the child plays the game, the more finer distinctions the child can make, far more distinctions than by simply reading about a subject. Always remember that nature multiplies by dividing. So the more and finer distinctions a person can make about a subject, the higher their intelligence.

How high is a Parent's or Teacher's IQ?

Young people today are tested enough, in school and out of school. In sharing the responsibility of children's intelligence growth, a parent or teacher also needs to test their own IQ (Interest Quotient) in their children's education. My highly educated dad, the Superintendent of Education, often said that parents also needed to take tests...tests that would measure their personal interest and activities. At parent teacher meetings, he recommended parents ask themselves questions such as these on a weekly basis and keep track of their scores. If the meeting got heated, he often handed out his "IQ Test For Parents." This is a copy of his test.

1. How many times per week do you ask your child, "Did you do your homework?" And then check on it and go over it with them. Or ask your child, "How is school going?" and take the time to actually find out. _____. (Many parents simply ask the questions but are not really interested in the answers.)

2. How many hours a week do you spend actually giving your child a hand with their homework? _____. (It's not

about giving them the answer but more about supporting them in the process of learning.)

3. How many hours a week do you spend actually playing with your child? _____. (Physically playing, practicing a sport together, and most importantly having active fun together.)

4. How many hours a week do you spend entertaining your child? _____. (Watching TV together, going to the movies, sporting events, taking family vacations.)

5. How many hours a week do you spend educating your child on subjects you think are important for their life-long development? _____. (Subjects such as spirituality, morality, finances, civic responsibility, helping the less fortunate, and leadership activities such as scouting.)

6. How many hours a week do you, the parent, spend on your own personal education? _____. (Reading non-fiction books, attending classes at local community colleges, reading professional publications, etc. My dad felt there were too many parents telling their children how important an education was but they themselves never continued their own education. He believed that actions spoke

louder than words.)

7. How well do you know your child's teachers? Do you respect them as people and as professionals? _____Yes_____ No. Are they the kind of role models you want for your children? _____Yes. _____ No. (It is not about criticizing, it is about being interested in the people who actually see your children as much as you do.)

8. How well do you know your child's friends and the parents of their friends? Do you respect them as people and as parents? _____ Yes _____No. Are they (the children and the parents) the kind of role models you want for your children? _____ Yes ___ No

9. Are you a role model of who you want your child to grow up to become? _____ Yes _____ No

10. How many times this week have you hugged your child? _____.

11. How many times this week have you told your child you loved him or her? _____.

12. How many times this week have you told your child that you were proud of him or her? _____.

My educated dad, often handed out this simple "IQ Test for Parents" as he called it, whenever the parents got up in arms about their children not doing well in school and blamed the teachers for the child's failure. He firmly believed that a child's most important teacher, good or bad, was ultimately the parent.

Education is a Family

Ultimately, a child develops his or her attitude for learning and education at home. This book and game were created in the hopes of developing a healthy attitude towards life-long learning. If CASHFLOW for KIDS inspires your children to learn more about the subject of money, and how to make even finer distinctions, then their lives will grow financially easier. So the process never ends…and as long as it never ends, your child's Financial IQ will only increase.

So does your child have a high financial IQ? Maybe and maybe not. Personally, I do not think how high your child's financial IQ is today is that important. What is important is whether or not your child is raised in an environment that encourages life-long learning so that your child's financial IQ continues to increase as he or she gets older.

A Note from Ann Nevin, Ph. D.

This chapter covers two very important breakthrough ideas in the history of educational psychology. First, you learned about IQ, intelligence quotients, and the change in thinking from IQ as a fixed quantity to the idea that there are many types of intelligences, with primarily verbal intelligence being promoted and valued in academic environments. Second, you were exposed to the idea of asking questions as a way of changing from one pattern of thinking to a new one. Robert's questions allow your mind to begin formulating your own answers even as you continue to read to find out what Robert will say about each question he poses. This model of teaching is a very powerful teaching tool.

There is power inherent in the process of asking questions. When you ask a question you are showing that you know enough to ask about a subject. When you ask a question instead of telling the answers (or making corrections when the children seem about to "make a mistake"), you show respect for the child's decisions. Questions allow children time to review the reasons they are making a decision. Questions that ask for predictions can give children the opportunity to exercise their imagination. Asking children to generate their own questions is another powerful teaching/learning technique, too. Questioning indicates the skill of 'critical thinking' and requires children to 'think about what they are learning' instead of blindly accepting 'facts.'

Thomas Armstrong, a famous scholar researcher in the area of multiple intelligence's, suggests that teachers should stop asking, "How smart is this child?" Instead he encourages teachers to ask, "How is this child smart?" Similarly, you can stop asking, "How smart am I?" and start asking, instead, "How am I smart?" Your mind immediately begins to search for different answers given the different questions. After completing this book and playing CASHFLOW for KIDS with your children, you may find yourself no longer asking, *"How financially intelligent am I?"* Your new question may be, *"How am I financially intelligent?"*

A Note From Sharon Lechter, CPA

The Game CASHFLOW for Kids

The basic educational principles that we utilized in developing CASHFLOW for KIDS can be summarized as follows:

1. Subjects are best learned at an early age.
2. The family's attitude about money is a very powerful influence on a child's attitude about money beginning at an early age.
3. Repetition enforces the learning process.
4. Making learning fun enhances the learning process.
5. Children learn best by involving multiple learning modalities.
6. There are different intelligences and hence different forms of genius.

CHAPTER 2
Building Block #1

Be Sure To Do Your Homework

Have You Done Your Homework?

"Have you done your homework?" my mom asked.

"I'll do it as soon as this game is over," was my reply.

"You've been playing long enough! Stop playing right now and hit the books. If you don't get good grades, you won't get into college, and then you won't get a good job," she scolded.

"OK. OK. I'll put the game away, but after I buy one more hotel."

"Listen to your mother and put that game away now."

That was my dad's voice and he did not sound happy. Knowing better than to ask for more time,

I stopped immediately and began putting the game away. It hurt me to sweep up my little green houses, red hotels, and property deeds I had spent hours collecting. I was close to controlling one whole side of the board. Yet I knew my parents were right. I did have a test the next day and I had not yet begun to study.

There was a period of my life when I was utterly fascinated by the game of "Monopoly." I played it regularly between the ages of eight and fourteen, which was the year I started playing high school football. I suspect I would have kept playing "Monopoly" regularly if I could have found more kids my age to play the game. But by the time you're in high school, it was not the cool thing to do. Although I played the game less frequently, I never lost my love of the game, and once I got old enough, I began playing the game in real life.

Building Blocks From My Rich Dad

The rest of this book is sectioned into building blocks. One of the most important was about homework.

In my previous books, I explained how I learned about money working for my rich dad from the age of nine into my college years. In exchange for my labor, he would spend hours teaching his son and me the ins and outs of running a business as well as the skills needed to be an investor. There was many a Saturday that I would have rather been surfing with my friends or playing some other sport, yet I often found myself sitting in my rich dad's office, learning from a man who would one day become one of the wealthiest private citizens in Hawaii.

During one of Saturday lessons, my rich dad asked Mike and me, "Do you know why I will always be richer than the people who work for me?"

Mike and I sat blankly for awhile, searching our minds for an appropriate answer. At first it seemed like a stupid question but knowing rich dad, we knew there was something important to learn from his question. Finally I ventured what I thought was the obvious answer. "Because you make more money than they do." I said.

"Yeah," Mike nodded in agreement. "After all you own the company and you decide how much you get paid and how much they get paid."

Rich dad rocked back in his chair grinning. "Well it is true that I decide how much everyone gets paid. But the truth is, I get paid less than many of the employees who work for me."

A frown came over my face and Mike looked at his dad with a suspicious gaze. "If you own this business, how can other people be paid more than you?" Mike asked.

"Well there are several reasons why," replied rich dad.

"So tell us." I said.

"Well, when starting up a business cash is often tight, and the owner is usually the last to be paid."

"You mean the employees always get paid first?" asked Mike.

Rich dad nodded his head saying, "That is

correct. And not only do they get paid first, they often get paid more than I do when I do get paid."

"But why is that?" I asked. "Why own a business if you get paid last and get paid the least?"

"Because that is what a business owner often needs to do at first if he plans to build a successful business."

"That makes no sense," I replied. "Tell me why you do it then."

"Because employees work for money and I work to build an asset," said rich dad.

"So as you build this business, your pay will go up?" Mike asked.

"It may and it may not. I say this because I want you to know the difference between money and an asset," rich dad continued. "I may or may not pay myself more later on, but I am not working hard for the paycheck. The reason I work hard is to build an asset that increases in value. I may someday sell this business for millions of dollars, or I may just hire a president to run it for me one day, and I will go on to build another business."

"So to you building a business is building an asset. And the asset is more important to you than money." I said doing my best to understand the distinction between money and the asset.

"That's right," said rich dad. "And the second reason I get paid less is because I already have other sources of income."

"You mean you have money from other assets?" I asked.

Rich dad nodded his head. "And that is the reason I asked you boys the question in the first place. That is why I asked you why I will be richer than my employees regardless of who makes the most money in salary. I am doing my best to teach you a very important lesson."

"And what is the lesson?" asked his son Mike.

"The lesson is you don't get rich at work. You get rich at home," said rich dad sternly, making sure we did not take his words lightly.

"I don't understand," I commented. "What do you mean you get rich at home?"

"Well, it's at work where you earn your money. And it is at home where you decide what you are going to do with your money. And it is what you do with your money after you earn it that makes you rich or poor." replied rich dad.

"It's like homework," said Mike.

"Exactly," said rich dad. "That is exactly what I call it. I call getting rich my homework."

"But my dad brings a lot of work home." I said almost defensively. "But we're not rich."

"Well your dad brings his work home, but he really does not do his homework," said rich dad. "Just as your mom does housework...that is not what I mean by homework."

"Or yard work." I added.

Rich dad smiled. "Yes, there is a difference between yard work and the kind of homework I am talking about." It was then my rich dad said something to me I have never forgotten. "The primary difference between the rich, the poor, and the middle class is what they do in their spare time."

"Their spare time," I said in a shocked tone.

"What do you mean their spare time?"

Rich dad smiled at his son and me for a moment. "Where do you think this restaurant business was started?" he asked. "Do you think that this business came out of thin air?"

"No," said Mike. "You and mom started this business at our kitchen table. That is where all your businesses have been started."

"That's correct," said rich dad. "Do you remember the small store we used to have years ago?"

Mike nodded his head. "Yes I do." said Mike. "Those were very tough days for the family. We had so little money."

"And how many stores do we have now?" asked rich dad.

"We own five," Mike replied.

"And how many restaurants?" asked rich dad.

"We own seven," said Mike.

As I sat there listening, I began to understand a few new distinctions. "So the reason you earn less from this restaurant is because you have income from many other businesses?"

"That is partly the answer," rich dad said with a grin. "The rest of the answer is found on this 'Monopoly' game board. Understanding the game of 'Monopoly' is the best kind of homework you can do."

"'Monopoly'?" I asked with a start. I could still hear my mom's voice telling me to put my 'Monopoly' game away and do my homework. "What do you mean 'Monopoly' is homework?"

"Let me show you," said rich dad as he opened

up the world's most familiar game. "What happens when you go around 'Go'?" he asked.

"You collect $200 dollars," I replied.

"So every time you go around "Go" that is like you collecting your paycheck. Is that correct?"

"Yeah. I guess so," said Mike.

"And to win the game, what are you supposed to do?" asked rich dad.

"You're supposed to buy real estate." I said.

"That's right," said rich dad. "And buying real estate is your homework. That is what makes you rich. Not your paycheck."

Mike and I sat there in silence for a long period of time. Finally I ventured a question to rich dad. "So are you saying a big paycheck does not make you rich?"

"That's correct," said rich dad. "A paycheck does not make you rich. It is what you do with that paycheck that makes a person rich, poor, or middle class.

"I don't understand," I said. "My dad is always saying that if he got a bigger pay raise we would be rich."

"And that is what most people think," said rich dad. "But the reality is that the more money most people make, the further in debt they get. So they have to work harder."

"And why is that?" I asked.

"It's because of what they do at home. It's what they do in their spare time," said rich dad. "Most people have a poor plan or a poor formula for their money after they make it."

"So where does a person find a good formula

for wealth?" Mike asked.

"Well, one of the better formulas for wealth is found right here on the 'Monopoly' board," rich dad said pointing to the game board.

"What formula?" I asked.

"Well, how do you win the game?" asked rich dad.

"You buy several pieces of real estate, then you begin putting houses on them," Mike answered.

"How many houses?" asked rich dad.

"Four," I said. "Four green houses."

"Good," said rich dad. "And after you have those four green houses, then what do you do?"

"You turn those four green houses in and buy a red hotel," I said.

"And that is one of the formulas for great wealth," said rich dad. "Right here on the game board of 'Monopoly', you have one of the best formulas for wealth in the world. It is a formula that many people have followed to become richer beyond their wildest dreams."

"You're kidding me," I said with a bit of disbelief. "It can't be that simple?"

"It's that simple," rich dad confirmed. "For years I have taken the money I have earned in my business and simply bought real estate. Then what I do is live off the income from my real estate and continue to build my businesses. The more money I make from my business, the more money I invest in real estate. That is the formula of great wealth for many people."

"So if it is so simple, why don't more people do it?" asked Mike.

"Because they don't do their homework," said rich dad.

"Is it the only formula for wealth?" I asked.

"No," said rich dad. "But it is a very sound plan that has worked for many wealthy people for centuries. It worked for kings and queens of old and it still works today. The difference is that today, you don't have to be nobility to own real estate."

"So you have been playing the game of 'Monopoly' in real life?" asked Mike.

Rich dad nodded his head. "Years ago, I decided that my plan for great wealth was to build businesses and then have my businesses buy my real estate. And that is all I have been doing. Even when we had very little money, I was still going home and looking for real estate."

"Does it have to be real estate?" I asked.

"No," said rich dad. "But when you get older and begin to understand the power of corporations and tax law, you will understand why real estate is one of the best investments."

"What else can you invest in?" asked Mike.

"Many people like stocks and bonds." said rich dad.

"Do you have stocks and bonds?" I asked.

"Oh yes." said rich dad. "But I still have more real estate."

"Why?" I asked.

"Well, it's because my banker will give me a loan to buy real estate but he frowns on giving me a loan to buy stocks. So I can leverage my money better with real estate. But we're getting off the point."

"And what is the point?" I asked.

"The point is you get rich at home not at work," said rich dad. "I really want you to understand that. I don't care if you buy real estate or stocks or bonds or build a business. I do care that you understand that most people do not get rich at work. You get rich at home by doing your homework."

"I got the lesson." I said. "So when you finish working here at the restaurant, where do you go next?"

"Glad you asked," said rich dad. "Come on. Let's get in my car and take a ride. I'll show you where I go after work is done."

A few minutes later we arrived at a large tract of land with row after row of houses on the land. "This is twenty acres of prime real estate," rich dad said as he pointed to the land.

"Prime real estate?" I said with cynical suspicion. I may have only been 12 years old, but I knew a low rent neighborhood when I saw one. "This place looks terrible."

"Well let me explain something to you," said rich dad. "Think of these houses as those green houses on the Monopoly board. Can you see that?"

Mike and I nodded our heads slowly, doing our best to stretch our imaginations. The houses were not the neat clean green houses on the Monopoly board. "So where is the big red hotel?" we asked almost simultaneously.

"It's coming," said rich dad. "It's coming. But it's not going to be a red hotel. In a few years the town will grow out in this direction. There is a new airport going in on the other side of this property."

"So these houses and land will be between the town and the airport?" I asked.

"You got it," said rich dad. "Then when the time is right, I will tear down all these rental houses and convert this land into a light industrial park. And then I will control one of the most valuable pieces of land in this town."

"Then what will you do?" Mike asked.

"I will follow the same formula," said rich dad. "I'll buy more green houses and when the time is right turn them into red hotels, or light industrial parks, or apartment houses, or whatever the city needs at that time. I'm not a very smart man but I know how to follow a successful plan. I work hard and I do my homework."

Building Block One

In my book *Rich Dad Poor Dad*, rich dad's lesson number one was that the rich did not work for money. Instead, the rich focused on having their money work for them. As a young boy, I will always remember the impact of comparing the lesson from the game board of 'Monopoly' to the lesson in real life with my rich dad.

Once I returned from Vietnam in 1973, I immediately signed up for a real estate investment course I saw advertised on television. The course cost $385.00. That single course has made my wife and me millionaires, and the income from the real estate we bought using the formula taught by that course has bought us our freedom.

Today, although my wife and I never need to work again, we continue to build businesses and the income from our business buys more assets. Assets such as more businesses, real estate, or paper assets such as stocks, bonds, mutual funds, hedge funds, insurance, etc. But all of this wealth came from my rich dad's advice of "you don't get rich at work. You get rich at home." That is why you should do your homework.

A note from Ann Nevin, Ph.D.

Between the ages of 5 and 14, a child begins developing what we in Educational Psychology often refer to as the child's "Winning Formula." It's the formula that the child believes he or she can best win at the game of life. Obviously, it's a very important and delicate period of life and needs to be approached with great care and love.

For example, if a child should have a bad experience in school, that experience may set the tone for the rest of his or her school years. The child may make decisions on how he or she plans to "win" or "lose" in this environment called school. Many times if a child is labeled "stupid" or "slow" by either parent or instructor, the child may adopt the belief that he or she is not as smart as other children. The life-long consequences of such early events can be devastating.

On the positive side, if the child has a positive experience in school, and adopts a belief that he or she is smart and school will be easy, then that too will have it's own life-long consequences. The point being made is that these years are really important years. It is difficult to tell how a child will respond to positive and negative experiences. For example failing a test may cause a child to study harder, or that same experience may cause the child to lose interest in studying further. So that is why it is important to be observant and watch how a child responds to different situations, rather than lecture the child and tell him or her what to be doing or feeling.

In Robert's story, he had very positive associations about wealth from his rich dad. His rich dad took the time to instruct verbally, had the two boys play the game of 'Monopoly', and then he took them to actually see and touch the real "green houses that were soon to be red hotels." It is obvious that between the ages of 5 and 14, Robert developed his winning formula of building businesses and investing in real estate, a formula he continues to use today.

So the years between 5 and 14 are very important years. As an educational psychologist I would say that what is most important during this period is that a child feel loved and have fun. All too often today, parents are pressuring their children to "perform" in school. They want their children to achieve good marks so they can get into the right college. While I know that education is important, excessive pressure to perform can be damaging and backfire later in life. A child may rebel later. Excessive rebellion in teenage years is often a form of delayed communication.

The problem with raising children is that there is not one formula that works for all children. That is why, during these early developmental years, observing, loving, and having fun with your children is crucial. If your child bonds with you during these years, you have a better chance of being bonded for life. If a child is bonded with love and respect, the chances are better that the child will listen to your advice as he or she gets older.

A note from Sharon Lechter:

Robert is accurate in saying that you don't get rich at work. As a CPA, I have assisted many people with their finances, particularly at tax time. This gives me the opportunity to see how different people have spent their time and their money. No two people spend their time and money in the same way. The primary difference between the rich, the poor, and the middle class is not how much money they earn but how wisely they spend their time and money at home. Simply stated, poor people, regardless of how much money they make, spend everything they make. The middle class tend to spend more than they make by going deeper into debt with each pay raise. And the rich focus on being good stewards of money, keeping as much as they can, protecting it, and having it grow for future generations.

Robert's story discusses the importance of homework. The idea of starting a business at home is an important first step for anyone who wants to achieve great wealth. The reason a home business is important is because it allows people to take advantage of the same tax strategies that the rich business owners enjoy. It is difficult for a CPA to do any kind of significant tax strategy work for a person who is an employee with only wage income. In fact in America, an employee, regardless if he or she is a janitor or president of the company, does not need a CPA if a salary is his or her only source of income. I would often recommend people keep their day-time job but start a part-time business at home, so they can start to take advantage of the same tax advantages that business owners enjoy. This is what Robert refers to as homework. In other words, it's OK to work for a big corporation but it is also important to own your own corporation.

I also caution you, however, not to form a corporation just to avoid taxes. It would be illegal if your intent is simply to avoid taxes. The most important thing when starting a home business is to first have the intent to build a legitimate business that will be profitable and then look for ways to minimize taxes on the income it generates. If you do create a profitable business at home, a CPA can be of great assistance to you. If you create a home based business and it is not profitable, a CPA can be less help. So think carefully about starting your own home based business. Always seek advice from people who have already done what you want to do and have done it successfully.

Next, Robert will discuss the differences between employees, business owners, the self-employed and investors. He will be analyzing the four different types of people found in the world of business. From an accountant's point of view, knowing the differences between these four quadrants is important because the tax laws are different for income derived from each of the four quadrants. In the real world, the tax laws are typically written in favor of business owners and investors usually to the exclusion of employees and the self-employed. And as we all know, taxes are one of our greatest expenses. Knowing the subtle distinctions between the different quadrants is important not only for you but for your children. These four quadrants and their related tax strategies are not taught in school so it is important you learn about them at home. As Robert's rich dad said, "You get rich at home, not at work. That is why you should do your homework."

CHAPTER 3
Building Block #2

Choose What You Want To Be When You Grow Up

My educated dad often said "Go to school, get good grades, and find a safe secure job, with good pay and excellent benefits."

My rich dad offered different advice. He would say, "I recommend you learn to build businesses, but more importantly learn to be an investor."

In my book, *The CASHFLOW Quadrant*, which is book two of the *Rich Dad Poor Dad* series, it was my rich dad who introduced me to the following diagram.

For those who may not have read this book, I will quickly review the thoughts behind the CASHFLOW Quadrant.

1. The E stands for employee.
2. The S stands for self-employed which includes small business owners.
3. The B stands for business owner.
4. The I stands for investor.

In the book, I go into some of the key emotional, technical, and philosophical differences between each of these four different roles that make up the world of business. After reading the book, many people realize why different people tend to gravitate to different quadrants.

Since my rich dad recommended I learn to be a business owner, he often said, "If you want to be a great "B," a business owner, you must learn how to work with people in all four quadrants." He also said, "You can identify which quadrant a person is in by listening to their words." Rich dad then gave me the following examples."

1. A person who tends to be from the "E" quadrant will often say, "I'm looking for a safe, secure job." or, "What are the benefits?" Or, "When will I get a raise?" Rich dad said, "This person's core value is often the need for job security, low risk, and a steady paycheck."

2. A person from the "S" quadrant will often be heard saying something like, "My hourly rate is $100 per hour," Or "My commission is 6% of the entire sales price." These people also say, "Time is money." The reason they think this way is because they are basically selling their services. My rich dad would say, "These people think they have a business but they really own a job." The reason he said this was because if this person stopped working, their income would also stop. Rich dad said, "The difference between an "S" business owner and a "B" business owner is that a "B" business owner could leave their business for a year or more and come back to find the business more profitable and running better than when they left it. He also said that an "S" person's core value is often the need for independence, a need to be their own boss, a rebel, or a perfectionist.

The theme song for this type of person could be, "Nobody does it better," or Frank Sinatra's hit, "I did it my way." Because of that my rich dad also added that the "S" could stand for Solo, Stud,

Superman, Superwoman, Stubborn, and often Slave to their business."

Often, when a person says "I'm going to quit my job and start my own business", the individual actually migrates from the "E" quadrant to the "S" quadrant, while thinking he or she is headed for the "B" quadrant. This is why it is important to teach a child at an early age the distinctions between the different quadrants. There are great differences between each quadrant and too many people wind up as "S" quadrant people instead of being "B" quadrant people, which they intended to become. The saying that a journey of 1000 miles begins with a single step needs to be updated. The journey of a 1000 miles should begin with first an idea of where you want to go, before you travel a 1000 miles in the wrong direction, or to the wrong quadrant as it is in this case.

In many ways, the "S" could also stand for small business, which makes up a large and important segment of the economy. Many small retail shops, restaurants, trades, and professions fall into the "S" quadrant. Even though they think they own a business, there are great differences between "S" business owners and "B" business owners.

One distinction between a person in the "B" quadrant versus the "S" quadrant is that a "B" quadrant person owns a system...and that system does the work with or without the owner's participation. A "B" person works on creating a great system and finding great people to run the system. A very sophisticated "B" type person will follow the golden rule of business which is to use OPT and OPM, which stand for "Other People's Time" and "Other People's Money" to do their work for them.

Some of the more famous "B's" are Thomas Edison, founder of General Electric, Henry Ford, founder of Ford Motor Company, Bill Gates, founder of Microsoft, and Anita Roddick, founder of the Body Shop. While these people stayed and continued working in their businesses after the businesses were up and running, they could have left the companies if they chose to. As you know Ford and Edison eventually left, and their companies continue on today.

People in the "I" quadrant have their money work hard for them. A person in this quadrant is often seeking what is referred to as ROI, or return on investment. In *The Cashflow Quadrant*, there is an explanation of the seven different levels and types of investors.

The way you know which quadrant you are in is simply by taking note of which quadrant your cash flow comes from. For my wife and me, our income comes from the B and I quadrants.

Birds of a Feather

An important point to stress at this moment is the idea that people will gravitate to different quadrants. Saying it another way, the people in each quadrant are often very different from people found in other quadrants. When they say that "Birds of a feather flock together, it also applies to people in different quadrants flocking together", either as friends or by professional association.

Who Pays The Most in Taxes

Not only are the people different, but the laws for business and investing are also different for each quadrant. For example, the tax laws are very different for people in different quadrants...the worst quadrant being the "E" quadrant when it comes to taxes. As Sharon Lechter stated at the end of the last section, a person solely in the "E" quadrant in America really does not need a CPA for tax planning because there are very few tax strategies available for a person in the "E" quadrant.

Unfortunately many people are stuck in the "E" quadrant all their lives and therefore have little flexibility when it comes to tax planning. This tax inequality really frustrated my highly educated dad who was a life-long "E". My educated dad would make a lot of money and then go to his CPA for advice on how to save taxes. All the CPA could say to him was "Buy a bigger house for the interest tax deduction." To which my dad would reply, "But I'm paying too much interest already. I don't want to get deeper into debt and spend more money, I simply want to pay less in taxes."

Adding to his frustration, my poor dad also knew that my rich dad was making more money than he was and paying less in taxes. Since my school teacher dad was not aware of the different tax laws for income from the different quadrants, he really could not understand the reasons why he earned less and paid more in taxes. He often got angry and said, "I keep saying that the rich are crooks. Here I work so much harder, earn less money and yet I pay more in taxes." Again, financial IQ means making subtle distinctions about different financial subjects. And knowing the distinctions between the tax laws of the four different quadrants is important for anyone wanting to manage his or her finances wisely.

It was because of these great differences in taxes between quadrants that my rich dad often said, "Taxes are your largest expense and people in the "E" and "S" quadrants have the least control over that expense. If you want to be rich, choose the quadrant that offers you the most control over your taxes. The government offers more tax incentives to individuals in the "B" and "I" quadrant...so I recommend you learn to work from those quadrants first."

"You Can't Do That Here"

When speaking about investing strategies or tax strategies to a mixed group of people, I often have people object and say, "You can't do that here"…even though I am doing what they say I cannot do, exactly where they say I can't do it. One of the first questions I ask them is which quadrant they currently earn most of their income from.

I remember coming home from school and saying to my educated dad, "Hey Dad, Mike's dad just bought three houses for no money, and then sold them for twice as much as he paid for them. He made nearly $20,000 in less than three days.

On top of that, he says he does not have to pay any taxes on the gains."

My dad whose gross annual income was not much more than $20,000 at that time in the 1960's, put down his paper and said, "You can't do that. That's against the law." He then picked up his newspaper and kept reading. While still in high school I had learned a valuable life lesson, and that lesson was...Just because someone says "You can't do something." doesn't mean you can't. It just means that they can't. They may not be from the same quadrant.

Distinctions:

1. My highly educated dad was only aware of the "E" quadrant. Job security was a high priority for him. He was not aware of the "I" quadrant, nor did he think investing was an important subject. He believed in striving for a government pension and a pension from the teacher's union. That paradigm, or set of rules, is what caused him to say, "Get good grades so you can get a safe, secure job." A safe, secure job was priority number one...and his only priority. He had the strong middle class value of working hard for a big company or the government and working your way up the ladder. My rich dad encouraged his son and me to own the ladder. Instead of working for a corporation, he wanted us to own our own corporations. Instead of looking for a job, he wanted us to provide jobs. And to do so, we needed to

make finer distinctions about the different educational requirements of the different quadrants.

2. My rich dad encouraged me to learn to become an investor before leaving school. He wanted me to have a plan for what to do with my money before I earned it. Repeating what he often said, "If you don't have a plan for your money, then there are many people who will have a plan for it."

Rich dad would often say to me, "The trap that most people fall into is the trap of earning a paycheck in the "E" quadrant, then buying a house and having kids. Soon, they're earning more and more money, paying more and more in taxes, and getting further into debt. Soon it is true when this type of person says, "I can't afford to invest. I am making too much money and I have too many bills to pay." He would go on to explain that the very same person who initially said, "I don't have to worry about investing, I'm still young," is often the same person who winds up saying, after all the kids are gone and the house is paid off, "I'm too old to invest. It won't do any good because there is not enough time left in my life." In explaining investing, rich dad would say, "Investing is a function of time and money. If you start early, you have a lot of time and you will not need much money. If you start late, you have little time and you will need much more money. So start early. Begin learning to invest before you begin learning how to get deeper and deeper into debt."

3. Become an investor first, start your career second. My teacher dad often said, "I'll never be rich because I am a teacher, and teachers don't get paid much." My rich dad said, "If you are first an investor, you can be anything you want to be and still be financially free." I believe this distinction to be a very important one because I have often heard parents say to their children such things as, "Don't be a social worker because social workers don't make much money." Or "I don't care if you want to be a dancer, be a doctor because doctors make more money." My rich dad encouraged me to first become an investor because as an investor, I could then pursue any career I wanted to, without regard to how much the job paid. He would say, "Be an investor first and you can choose to do what you want because you love doing it, rather than because of how much it pays."

After playing "Monopoly", my rich dad would take me to see, touch, and feel his real green houses and red hotels. In retrospect, it was the relationship between the game and real life houses that had a tremendous impact upon my choice of quadrants before I was 12 years old.

After showing me his investment houses, he would constantly have me see, touch and feel all aspects of his multiple businesses. He often said, "The reason I am a business owner is because I like the freedom it gives me to invest, but also a well run business gives me the money to buy all the investments I want. After all, the main reason for having a business is for that business to buy my assets. Many people cannot afford to buy real estate because real estate is so capital and time intensive. A business gives me the money and the time to acquire my real estate and paper assets."

For those of you who read *Rich Dad Poor Dad*, you may remember the story about Ray Kroc, the founder of McDonald's. He had made a statement that his business was not hamburgers, but real estate. My rich dad had exactly the same train of thought.

When I talk to rich parents, I often find they physically have their children invest their own money, or even go to a stock brokerage house to anchor the learning experience. Many of their children have sizeable investment portfolios that they personally manage, even before they leave high school.

I was watching television the other night, and there was a special program entitled, "Sons and Daughters at the Office." It was a special program being run in U.S. cities which was encouraging parents to bring their children to the office to show them what mom or dad did all day. There was also another program that showed the child-care center at the office so the parents could stay close to the child. That reinforces the "E" quadrant much more than the "I" quadrant. The parents seemed happy with the programs because to most of them job or professional security remains their primary focus, the core value of the "E" quadrant.

So the choice is really up to the parents as to which quadrant they want to educate their children to focus on first. By playing CASHFLOW for KIDS, the parent is beginning to make the child aware of the differences between the four quadrants and the different types of income each quadrant generates. By playing CASHFLOW for KIDSearly, the parent is reinforcing the importance of becoming an investor at an early age.

My rich dad once wrote these words.

Poor and Middle class priorities

1. Employment security
2. Consumption for life's comfort
3. Savings
4. Investing (if there is anything left over)

A rich person's priorities.

1. Investment portfolio
2. Professional satisfaction
3. Savings
4. Consumption for life's comfort

And then he said, "The rich are not necessarily

smarter, they just have different priorities. So today, the question is, "Do you want to teach your children the priorities of the rich, or the priorities of the poor and middle class?"

So in summary, my poor dad said this quadrant was the first quadrant to learn:

My rich dad said this quadrant was the first quadrant to learn:

Comments from Ann Nevin, Ph.D.

Knowing what you want to be when you grow up can become a life's goal or priority. Having choices about one's goals and priorities is an important aspect of self-determination, and choosing a direction in life. The most creative people I know are those who are very self-determined individuals. They are constantly setting goals and priorities, achieving them, celebrating their achievement, and then setting new goals and priorities. Their creativity is spurred and expanded every time they repeat this learning cycle.

CASHFLOW for KIDS has been designed to teach children the skills needed to be successful in the B and I quadrants. The game takes advantage of the latest teaching technology that allows children to be active learners and goal setters. The game also takes advantage of a teaching/learning principle based on the power of natural consequences. Players have a chance to experience what happens when they make specific decisions. It teaches them to make finer distinctions about money and about life skills.

Anticipation of consequences (both desired and undesired) occurs when you ask children to predict "What might happen if you buy this, or sell this, or pay this bill?" In other words, every time your child does something with money, by looking at their financial statement, they will be able to see the "ripple effect" of their actions...both short term and long term. After they have had a chance to do: "such and such", ask them "What did you learn by doing such and such?" and 'What might you do differently in the future?" This gives your child meaningful practice in making financial plans, a lifelong skill which will continue to grow in value. They will learn that in life there are not linear lines, or just right and wrong answers. They will be able to see the ripple effect of their financial decisions and that each decision has multiple consequences in life. In school there may be only one "right" answer. But in real life, there are multiple answers radiating from each decision we make. That is vital for a child to learn at as early as possible.

Comments From Sharon Lechter

CASHFLOW For KIDS was created to teach children the priorities of the rich. It teaches that salary income is "you working for money" (from the "E" and "S" quadrants) and that income generated by your assets in the form of passive income is "your money working for you" (from the "B" and "I" quadrants). It shows the benefits of buying assets and keeping expenses low.

All players begin the game as employees with the same amount of salary income and expenses. Through game play they quickly learn that by buying assets they can increase their passive income. Once their passive income exceeds their expenses, they are financially free and become a CASHFLOW Kid!

An object of this game is to have young people learn to think like "B's" and "I's". And what "B's" or "I's" do is convert their paycheck into assets that generate cash flow. If a person has income from assets instead of a job, they feel more secure about life. In the game, the players may be faced with losing their jobs and therefore their salaries for a number of turns. The impact of losing their salary is less severe if the players have passive income as well. Even though they have lost their salary, they do not stop receiving their passive income. So the children begin to learn not to live in fear of losing their jobs, or spending their lives clinging to job security. If a child knows how to be an "E" or an "S" and how to spend his or her money like a "B" or an "I" he or she will have a life of financial security and financial self-confidence.

One of the problems with people young and old is that they spend their money on things that lose value the moment you buy them. Kids today spend much of their time learning about money management from retailers. In the game of CASHFLOW for KIDS, these things that lose value immediately are called "doodads." In real life, the reason most people suffer financially is not because they do not earn enough money. They suffer because they spend their money foolishly. They do what we accountants call, "Turning cash to trash."

As Ann Nevin said the game and the use of financial statements gives the child a picture of the "ripple effect" of each financial transaction. Since most adults are also not financially literate, they cannot see the "ripple effect" of their own financial actions. For example, if a person receives a raise and impulsively runs out to buy a new lake house on credit they often fail to realize the ultimate impact of that pay raise to their financial statements. They fail to see that even though the raise increases their income, their decision to purchase the lake house has created a new liability (mortgage) with a related monthly expense (mortgage payment). Since the lake house is not generating income, the net result after taking taxes into effect is that they have increased their liabilities (which takes money out of their pocket) and not increased their assets (which would put money into their pocket). Add to this the monthly maintenance costs and increased taxes due to the higher income, and this couple may very well have less cash flow each month that they did before the raise as a result of their decision to purchase the lake house.

The object of the CASHFLOW games is to teach financial literacy, which would include being able to see the ripple effect from all your financial actions, big or small. As a CPA I love this game because it teaches kids what I wish so many adults (big kids) would know about financial intelligence and financial literacy. The reason I put "big kids" in parenthesis is because when it comes to money, especially pay raises or bonuses, too many adults act like big kids.

The fundamental difference between the rich and everyone else is that the rich buy assets first and luxuries second. The poor and middle class try to buy luxuries first and never have money to buy assets. By focusing on buying more and more assets the rich are able to have their assets buy their luxuries. People in the "E" and "S" quadrants often have to work harder and harder to pay off the debt from living in a life of luxury.

A simple yet important thing your children can learn from playing CASHFLOW for KIDS is to set priorities. If they learn to buy assets first, their life will be financially secure. If they learn to buy luxuries first, they will most likely be relegated to a life of hard work just to pay the bills.

As a parent, you have an opportunity to take the time to understand the differences between the income from the four different quadrants and how they can have a long-term impact on you and your child's financial security. When you advise your child to get a safe, secure job, please think about the long-term tax consequences of such advice.

The point of this book and this game is for your child to have the knowledge to choose which quadrant they want to work from. To choose to operate out of the "B" and "I" quadrants, your child will need financial skills not taught in school. The game CASHFLOW for KIDS has been created to teach your child the basic financial skills required to be successful in the "B" and "I" quadrants.

CHAPTER 4
Building Block #3

Know the 3 Different Kinds of Income

In my book *Rich Dad Poor Dad*, I told a story about my first job working for my rich dad at the age of nine. In that story, I was stacking canned goods in one of his small convenience stores. He paid me ten cents an hour. After working for a while, I went to him and asked for a raise. Instead of a raise, he took my ten cents away and informed me that I would now work for free...which I did.

Of all the stories in that book, that story drew many interesting comments. A medical doctor friend of mine said that he was ready to put the book down at that moment and go looking for my rich dad to give him a piece of his mind. Thank goodness he continued reading and found out the long-term value of the lesson my rich dad was teaching me...that lesson being, "The rich don't work for money." His complete lesson was that the rich knew how to have money work for them. That is what made the rich, rich. Not a big paycheck or pay raises.

More financially technical, the lesson he was teaching me was the distinctions between the three different types of income. Some years later, when I was more able to understand the subtle distinctions about income, money, accounting, and taxes, rich dad said to me,

"There are three types of income. They are earned income, passive income, and portfolio income. If you want to be rich you want to work hard to convert earned income into passive and or portfolio income. If you have passive and portfolio income, that means your money is working for you, rather than you working for it."

He went on to explain that of all the three types of income, earned income was the most heavily taxed. That was because earned income came primarily from the E and S quadrants. The least taxed income, or more importantly the income over which you have the most control regarding the taxes you pay, came from portfolio income and passive income.

Portfolio income is income generally from paper assets such as stocks, bonds, and mutual funds. Passive income is income generally derived from real estate.

One of the reasons, and there are many, why

my rich dad had me work for free was because he never wanted me to become what he called "addicted" to earned income. He would say "Earned income is you working for money...and rich people do not work for money." By taking away my ten cents per hour wage, he was beginning to teach me to learn to acquire passive income and portfolio income.

Instead of telling me to stop playing "Monopoly", he encouraged me to play the game as often as I could. In some of the Saturday classes, he would occasionally break out his game and play against his son and me, using the game as a teaching tool about passive income. I remember him saying, "What you are learning by playing 'Monopoly' is one of the most important formulas for wealth there is. It is a simple formula, but it is a formula that has made people like me very, very wealthy. Play this game, learn the formula of start small, buy one green house, and then another, until you have four green houses. Then convert the green houses into a red hotel. If you will do that in real life, slowly but surely you will amass tremendous wealth. Always remember that real estate is an important basis of real wealth."

My rich dad would go on to explain that portfolio income, which is most often income from paper assets, was excellent income also. He would say, "There are different pros and cons to the different incomes. Stocks and bonds are easier to buy and sell and are less of a headache to manage than real estate. And you can often get rich much more rapidly from paper assets. Real estate has much better tax advantages than paper assets and banks love to give me long-term low interest loans to buy it.

During one Saturday class with rich dad, I asked him "Which is better? Stocks or real estate?" His reply was, "Both are better. Both have advantages and both have disadvantages. Both have similarities and both have differences. Your job is to learn how to handle both types of assets. Learn how to handle those two assets and you will learn how to acquire passive income and portfolio income." Rich dad went on to say, "If you want to be financially intelligent, you need to learn how to invest in both real estate as well as paper assets."

Somebody has Plans for Your Money

One day during a Saturday game of "Monopoly" with rich dad, I told him about my dad telling me to put the game away and to do my homework. Rich dad listened to my story intently and then said, "If you want to be rich, you must have two plans. One plan is how you plan to earn money. The second plan is what you plan on doing with your money after you earn it. Of the two plans, the second plan is the most important."

Being confused I asked him, "What do you mean two plans?"

Rich dad thought for a moment and then said slowly, "When your dad told you to put the game away and do your homework, he was asking you to work on plan one."

"Plan one?" I repeated back in confusion.

"When he says, 'get good grades so you can get a good job,' he is giving you good advice on how to get a good job so you can earn money."

"But he doesn't have a plan two." Mike added. "Which is what you focus on."

Rich dad nodded his head. "If you don't have a plan for your money, then there are millions of people who do. And because most people have no real plan for what to do with their money after they make it, they end up with money problems."

"So the reason you have me play "Monopoly", is because you want me to know what to do with my money before I start making it."

Rich dad nodded his head. All too often you hear people saying such things as, "I know I should save but I just don't have any money left to save." Or they say, "I know I should invest, but investing is too risky." These are symptoms of people who learned how to make money, which is plan one, but never really had a plan two. And because they did not have a plan two, other people did have plans for their money."

"So playing 'Monopoly' is a very important part of our education?" I asked excitedly. I was excited because I wanted an excuse to play the game more and more.

"Yes it is." said rich dad. "And so is going to school. The most important thing to learn from this is that you need to have two plans for money."

"One plan is how to work so you can acquire earned income. Plan two is how to convert that earned income to passive and portfolio income." I said.

Rich dad nodded his head. "In fact, I would recommend that once you graduate from college and begin earning money, instead of focusing on earning more earned income, I suggest that you focus on how to have more passive income and portfolio income before you're forty. To be rich and financially free by age forty would be a great goal. And to do that, you will need passive income and portfolio income."

CASHFLOW for KIDS was designed to teach your children how to convert earned income into passive income and portfolio income. Cashflow 101 and 202 were designed to teach adults the more sophisticated ways of converting earned income into passive and portfolio income.

How Soon should Children have a Plan for the Money They Make?

A short time ago, I taught a class of 15 year-old students in San Francisco. These were bright students from poor families that had been gathered together in an innovative new school. During my talk on financial literacy, I asked the class, "What are you going to do when you finish school?"

Immediately, a young man raised his hand and shouted out, "I'm going to get a high paying job and buy a flashy new car. After that, I'll get married, have kids, and live in a big fancy house." Most of the class clapped and nodded in agreement.

After the clapping subsided, I then asked, "What about investing your money?"

The same young man waved his hand at me in

a slapping down motion. "Oh man, you want me to miss out on life. I don't have to think about investing. Besides, I'm still young."

When I am asked, "How young should a child be to have a plan for the money they are about to make?" I think back to that young man and his classmates. It was obvious that the young man already had a plan on what he was going to do with the money he was going to make and most of that money was going to go to somebody else. So my rich dad's answer would be, "The sooner the better. If you don't talk to your child about what to do with their money, there are many other people who will."

Note from Ann Nevin, Ph.D.

CASHFLOW for KIDS has been designed to take advantage of the latest teaching technology that allows children to be active learners. CASHFLOW for KIDS is self-paced allowing children to move onto the next level when they are ready. CASHFLOW for KIDS sets your child up to learn in a fun action oriented game rather than through boring worksheets.

Playing CASHFLOW for KIDS with your child will give you and your child tangible and vivid experiences. These experiences will give you concrete examples to explain the financial concepts being played out in the game. Your child acquires a direct physical relationship between the concepts as the game is played. You will want your child to play this game over and over again. Playing this game and being an active learner will make it possible for your child to learn quickly, easily, and with much stronger memory.

A Note From Sharon Lechter, CPA

CASHFLOW for KIDS:
1. There are three different types of income.
   a. Earned - You working for money
   b. Passive - Your money working for you
   c. Portfolio - Your money working for you

CASHFLOW for KIDS is designed to teach the differences between these three different incomes. While playing the game with the child, a little positive reinforcement about being a smart young person who knows the difference between the three will go a long way in life. In real life, most adults are not aware of the three different types. Most people think that all incomes are equal.

2. The need for two plans for your money.
   a. One plan to make money.
   b. One plan on what to do with the money after you make it.

Most people have some pretty definite plans on how they will make their money. That is why you often hear people say, "I'm going to focus on my career," or "I'm going to work my way up the corporate ladder." or "As soon as I have some money saved up, I'm going to start my own business." While playing CASHFLOW for KIDS with your children, remember to discuss the importance of knowing what to do with your money is as important as their plans on how they plan to earn *their money. The sooner your children think of investing as part of their plan to keep their money, the sooner it will become a reality.*

CHAPTER 5
Building Block #4

Create Your Own Report Card

I remember the worst day of school was the day that the report cards came out. Although I scored above average on my Scholastic Aptitude Test I was an average to poor academic student. I would have loved to have hidden my report cards and not told my parents about them, but my dad was the head of education for the state, and he knew when they came out, so the moment my dad got home he would ask, "Where is your report card?"

All through school my grades were average to below average. Every time my mom saw my less than stellar grades, she would say the same thing. "Readers are leaders and leaders are readers. If you would read more your grades would be better." Of course I knew she was right, but I really was not interested in reading the books my teachers wanted me to read.

My mom was a great mom. She was extremely kind, always hugging her children as well as all of our friends. And she worried about us and our future. That is why she constantly reminded us to read books—although she rarely read books herself.

My highly educated dad, on the other hand, was an avid reader. I would say that he read a book a week, both fiction and nonfiction. Although he rarely encouraged us to read, he inspired us more by example than by words. And when it came to my less than impressive grades, he really said very little. If my mother nudged him to talk to me about my grades my dad would only say, "Try better next quarter." For my dad, good grades were not an issue. For my mom they were.

When I began spending more and more time with my best friend Mike and his father, my rich dad, both my parents became concerned. They were concerned because my rich dad had not finished high school, was not from the "right-side" of the tracks, and was a businessman as well as an investor. My highly educated parents were concerned about the influence he would have over me.

One night, when I had just turned 15 years of age, my dad asked me to sit next to him in his tiny and cramped reading room. Putting down his book my dad paused for a moment, took a deep breath and began by saying, "Son, your mom and I are both concerned about you spending so much time with Mike and his dad."

I was a little shocked and confused. "Why?" I asked.

"Well, you are spending more and more time with them. You and Mike go surfing and then you spend time in his dad's office. You also spend a little too much time working for his dad on the weekends."

"What is wrong with that?" I asked.

"We're concerned about what kind of influence he is on your life," my dad said softly. "We think you should be spending more time with other kids doing what other kids are doing."

"You mean sitting around smoking and hanging around the shopping mall," I replied sarcastically. "I don't want to do that."

"No. That is not what I mean," my dad replied. "Both your mom and I are glad you don't smoke and go to the mall all day. What we are concerned about is the fact that Mike's dad didn't complete school. He doesn't read much because I suspect he's not very literate, and we feel he may have a negative impact upon your future. Besides, he doesn't have a steady job and he is known in town as a real estate slum lord."

I could not believe what I was hearing. It took me a moment to gather my thoughts and then I began responding slowly. "Mike's dad spends more time with me than the two of you do because he doesn't have a job. He has a lot of free time because he owns businesses and invests in real estate. He knows that word literacy which is taught in school is important. He encourages Mike and me to study hard in school. But he is teaching me financial literacy, which is also important to know if I want to someday own my own businesses and become an investor. And while you call him a slum lord, he calls himself a provider of low income housing."

2 Different Worlds

Around the age of 15, I became acutely aware of two very different worlds. One world was the world of my mom and dad. Most of their friends and family members were government officials, school administrators, or college professors. Most were highly educated, well read, and prided themselves for being public servants or educators. At their parties, the conversation was about government funding, grants, pay raises, tenure, sabbaticals, leaves of absences, promotions, titles, and benefits. Most were sincerely dedicated to the social good of society.

The other world was my rich dad's world. A world filled with business owners, bankers, attorneys, accountants, brokers, investors, and other members of the deal-making world. At their parties, the conversations revolved around the market, P/E ratios, new issues, I.P.O.'s, real estate subdivisions, the problems with having employees, taxes, changes in tax law, politicians, and who made the most money.

One of the benefits of having two different words to associate with was that I grew to understand both worlds. I saw the value of both sides, as well as the limitations. I also noticed the difference between people who were financially literate and the people in academics who were predominantly word literate. I understood the Socialist view of life and also the Capitalist's view on the world. I noticed it in the cars the people drove to the party. One party had old Chevrolets out front and the other had new Cadillacs. Most importantly, I noticed that both sides seemed to be very happy with what they were doing professionally. Each group was also very suspicious of the other group. The government employees and college educators distrusted the business people. The business people complained about government officials, government waste, and schools that failed to train qualified employees. Yet rising above these petty differences I did come to appreciate the importance of both word literacy and financial literacy. It made the lessons and values learned from both groups of people priceless.

The Basis of Financial Literacy

Our educational system focuses predominantly upon word literacy. As stated earlier, a high IQ often refers to a person who is gifted in word literacy. Unfortunately, our educational system offers little to nothing on the subject of financial literacy. In my opinion, both types of literacy are important today. Today workers are more free agents rather than long term employees. And in a world of free agency more than job security, both word literacy and financial literacy are important.

My book *Rich Dad Poor Dad*, was

predominantly a book about financial intelligence with the basis of financial intelligence being financial literacy. The following diagram, the diagram of the Income Statement and the Balance Sheet is the basis of financial literacy.

The lack of financial literacy causes three main problems.

Problem #1: Not knowing the difference between an asset and a liability.

In *Rich Dad Poor Dad*, the statement that your home is not an asset caused quite a stir. Some people could not get past this one issue because it was contrary to one of their core beliefs. For those who may have not read the book, here is the reasoning behind that statement.

My educator dad always said, "Our home is an asset and our biggest investment." My rich dad did not disagree that the home was an investment, he just disagreed whether or not it was an asset at that moment. His reply was, "Your dad's home is not an asset and if it is his largest investment, your family is in big financial trouble."

My rich dad always said, "If you are financially literate, you can see which way the cash is flowing. When I look at a set of financial statements, I'm looking for the direction of cash flow. Cash flow in business and investing is everything. Cash flow is to a business owner and investor what blood flow is to the human body. If the body is hemorrhaging blood, the body is in trouble. The reason so many people and businesses are in trouble financially is because their cash flow is hemorrhaging. And the problem is, most people think that financial hemorrhaging is a normal way to live life." Rich dad went on to say, "When I read the numbers, the numbers tell me a story. By following the trail of cash flow, the story can be one of great wealth, a story of great financial tragedy, or a story of a lifetime of financial struggle. That is what reading the numbers tell me." He also said, "If you are financially literate, you do not have to take anyone else's opinion as to whether or not something is an asset or a liability. Because your dad is financially illiterate, he must have his banker and accountant do his reading for him. Although your father is a very smart man, he is not in control of his numbers. And if he is not in control of his numbers, he is not in control of his financial future."

At the age of nine, my rich dad began my education in financial literacy by showing me the cash flow pattern of an asset and a liability. The following diagrams of Income Statements and Balance Sheets show the cash flow patterns of an asset and a liability.

"This is the cash flow pattern of an asset. If you notice, the cash flows from the Asset Column into the Income Column." He would say. "An asset is something that puts money in your pocket.

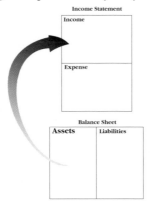

Finishing his simple drawings, he would say, "And this is the cash flow pattern of a liability." His simple definition of a liability for a nine-year-old was, "A liability is something that takes money from your pocket." He went on to say, "The reason your father's house is a liability is because your home takes money out of his pocket for the mortgage payment, taxes, and expenses.

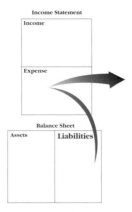

My rich dad was not saying not to buy a home. He was simply impressing upon me to call a liability a liability and an asset an asset. He said, "Your dad struggles financially simply because he calls liabilities assets." My rich dad went on and say, "Your dad works hard, and gets a pay raise. He then pays more in taxes. So he asks his accountant what he can do to reduce taxes. Since your dad earns his income from the 'E' quadrant, all the accountant can do is advise him to buy a bigger house because the government will give him a tax break on the interest he pays on the mortgage. So he buys a bigger liability, and the cash flows even faster out the expense column, and he continues to call it an asset. Add to that his car, his golf clubs, the furniture in the house, and other things he calls assets and soon he has no money left over at the end of the month with which to buy real assets. Most people's financial problems begin with not knowing the difference between assets and liabilities. So they spend their lives buying liabilities they think are assets. That is the problem with not being financially literate."

The point of this simple lesson is that a house can be an asset or a liability. The mistake many people make is in thinking that an asset or liability is a thing or an object. The abstract way of looking at the definition of an asset or liability is that the real asset or liability is not the asset, but more the person who is in control of the asset. For example, I buy a house and use it for a rental property. If after all expenses, mortgage and taxes are paid there is net income coming in from the rent then it is an asset. But if I should mismanage the same property, and fail to rent it for more than it costs me, then that same property becomes a liability. The same is true for anything we normally consider assets, such as gold, stocks, bonds, mutual funds. Anyone of these items could be either an asset or liability, simply by applying the cash flow acid test.

In other words, the real asset or liability is the person managing the alleged asset. And that is why learning the differences between an asset and a liability early in your life is very important. There are millions of people who are working hard to pay for liabilities they think are assets. And because that money is flowing out of their pockets, they have less money that could go to acquiring real assets. Real assets that could generate cash flow, which would make their lives financially easier. So by buying liabilities that they believe are assets, people become less financially secure and cling even harder to the idea of job security. They need job security to pay the monthly expenses for all those so called assets.

Problem #2: Not knowing how to recognize the distinctions between cash flow patterns.

My rich dad would say to me, "One look at a person's financial statement and I can tell if they are rich, poor, or middle class."

The Cash Flow Pattern of a Poor Person

The following are the diagrams he drew for me. The first diagram is the cash flow pattern of a poor person.

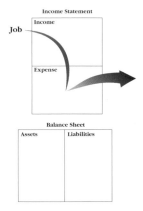

"A poor person is someone who spends everything he or she makes." Rich dad would say. "It has nothing to do with how much they make. I know many people who make a lot of money, but the problem is, they spend it as fast as it comes in. That is how they can be a poor person who makes a lot of money." Rich dad added, "This type of person often solves his or her financial problems by simply working harder. Often by taking a second job, or asking for overtime to earn more money."

The Cash Flow Pattern of a Middle Class Person

"This is a diagram of a middle class person."

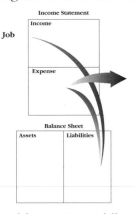

Rich dad would say, "A middle class person is a person who has long-term liabilities. They often only have income from a job. They have a mortgage, car payments, credit cards, etc. When these people say that they cannot afford to quit their job, they mean it." He would go on to say, "The problem with these people is that when they get a few extra dollars, they often spend that money to get further into debt. Let's say they receive a $5,000 bonus. Instead of investing it, they often use that money as a down payment on a new car or bigger home. This is how they become stuck in the rat race of life. They take their money and acquire bigger liabilities that they think are assets." Rich dad also said, "This group often solves their money problems by going further into debt. Instead of investing to create more income, they borrow either using credit cards, home equity loans, or bill consolidation loans to solve their financial problems.

The Cash Flow Pattern of the Rich

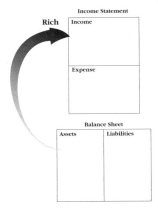

"This is the cash flow pattern of the rich." Rich dad said as he drew his diagrams. "Their income comes from the asset column, not a job or profession." The income that comes from the asset column is either passive income or portfolio income. Income that comes from a job or profession is earned income.

There are people who were fortunate to receive this income via inheritance. And then there are those who have had to create this income on their own through properly investing in assets.

Early in my life, I realized that my best friend, Mike, would be the one who would inherit an asset column worth tens of millions of dollars and I realized that I would be the one to start from scratch. Years later, when Mike realized that my asset column was accumulating some mass, he said, "I envy you. At least you did it on your own. My dad handed it to me." All I said was "I'd be happy to trade places."

The point is his dad trained us to both acquire assets as well as maintain the growth of the asset column. Keeping one's assets safe and growing is a technical science and an art in itself and should be taken seriously. If not, the money could be gone quickly. My accountant recently informed me that in America, the average life expectancy for an inheritance is about 18 months. In the few examples of people I know who have inherited money I can understand how that average could be true. An older business associate of mine died recently and left a sizeable estate to three of his children. Soon after the funeral, I noticed each one driving a new car, buying bigger homes, and taking lavish vacations. It's been a little more than 18 months but I doubt if the party will last much longer. I know the terms and conditions of his will, and I know that he did not leave the three of them enough to support their "Lifestyles of the newly rich and foolish."

Mike was well trained by his dad to take over the family fortune. Before he died, rich dad called all of his children together and informed them that Mike had control of the estate. He informed them that he was going to give the four of them their inheritance before he died. He gave each child three million dollars in cash. He said, "If you want to learn how to manage that money, Mike and I are willing to advise you. And if you don't want any financial advice, that is fine too. But don't come crying to me once the money is gone. That is a lot of money and it is up to you to do with it as you please." He then informed the kids that his businesses and investments belonged to Mike to continue to manage and to grow. It was all spelled out in the will and other legal documents. In less than five years, Mike's brothers and sisters were broke. The four kids went back to their father, my rich dad, and he informed them that the well had dried up. "I told you to ask for advice but none of you have," was all he said. Ten years after rich dad's death, Mike has done a spectacular job of growing the estate and keeping his brothers and sisters away from the goose that is laying the golden eggs. The court battles have begun.

The point of this lesson is that individuals who attain great wealth must put in place trustees or train their heirs to protect and grow the wealth. Parents who do not train their children well may find their children anxious for them to die, so their life can begin. My rich dad said that too many parents put provisions in their will that say, "My children will receive this money once they turn 25 or some other age." But they fail to teach them what to do with it after they receive it. That is why most great wealth is gone by the third generation."

A person who has the cash flow pattern of the

rich ingrained in their thought patterns will often invest money in assets to generate the money needed to solve their financial problems. Today whenever my wife and I want to buy a major luxury, we first acquire an asset. That asset will provide the cash flow to buy the luxury item. For example, when I wanted a new Porsche, we went out and bought a property that provided the cash flow to make the payments for the Porsche. Once the Porsche was paid off, we still had the asset and the cash flow with which to either reinvest or buy a new luxury.

The Point of Choice

I have heard many people say, "I'll never be rich because I don't make enough money." Or "It takes money to make money."

My rich dad taught me that how much money a person makes has little to do with whether or not they will be rich. He would say instead, "It's not how much money a person makes that makes them rich or poor. It's what a person does with what they make that makes them rich or poor."

The diagram on the next page is what rich dad called the "Point of Choice."

Rich dad would say, "At the point the money hits your hands, you have the power to determine your financial future. If you just spend it, you choose to be poor. If you acquire long-term debt that you must personally repay, you choose the financial pattern of the middle class. And if acquiring assets is your priority, then you choose the cash flow pattern of the rich."

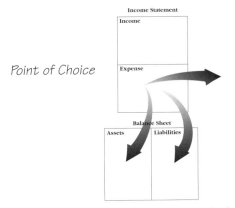

Point of Choice

These simple lessons have guided me over the years. I was not obsessed about getting the high paying job, or striving for the next promotion and pay raise. I knew that my financial destiny was not dependent upon my boss, a pay raise, the company, the economy, or luck. My rich dad impressed upon me that I could achieve great wealth without a high paying job. I knew my poor dad was not going to leave me any kind of inheritance, as my rich dad was going to leave his son. I knew that my financial destiny remained in my control. That certainty came from knowing which quadrant to earn my income in, taking control of my cash flow, having a plan on what to do with the money before I made it, and knowing the difference between an asset and a liability.

The Definition of Financial Intelligence

Rich dad's personal definition of financial intelligence was, "Financial intelligence is not about how much money you make. Financial intelligence is about how much money you keep, how hard that money works for you, and for how many generations you can keep that money." He would go on to say, "Financial intelligence begins with these simple diagrams of financial literacy. Financial literacy tells you the story about how you are managing your cash flow." While impressing upon me the importance of keeping my personal financial statements up to date and accurate, he would say, "Looking at your financial statement is like looking in a mirror. And when you look into the mirror, the question is "Are you looking at a rich kid, a poor kid, or a middle class kid? Only you have the power to determine who looks back at you." That is why he stressed that his son and I know what kind of cash flow pattern we were managing. At the age of 12, we knew that when we looked at our financials, we were looking into the future.

Distinctions

1. Word literacy is more important today, than ever before and so is financial literacy. My rich dad repeatedly said, "Those that are only word literate will work for those who are financially literate." In other words, it's the golden rule, which is "The person who has the gold makes the rules." And having the gold begins with financial literacy.

2. Having a high paying job is not as important as having personal control over your cash

flow. Too many people seem to be obsessed with how big their paycheck is. To be successful financially, we all need more financial education. And financial education begins with the basics of financial literacy. The fact is a young man working in a hamburger stand, earning a minimum wage, can become a millionaire while providing financial security for his family. All he needs is a little training that begins with education in financial literacy.

In San Francisco, while teaching that class of tough smart students from poor families, I explained to them that each of them held their financial destiny in their hand, with every dollar they touched. When I drew the diagrams of the cash flow patterns of the rich, the poor, and the middle class, the lights went on for a few of them. Several got very excited and others got very angry. Some of the teachers wanted to debate my definition of a house being a liability. Some of the teachers were concerned that if the young people knew that they could become wealthy without an education and a high paying job they would lose interest in school. Then the teachers would lose their leverage.

At a debriefing session with the teachers, I explained to the teachers that the students already know that they don't have to go to school to become successful. Everyday they are bombarded with examples of sports stars, movie stars, rock stars who are extremely rich but did not do well in school. I suggested they reexamine their objectives and their curriculum, and bring it into the 21st century. In closing I said, "Many of these students will not go on to college. You and I know that. And if they do go on to college, do you think that corporate America will welcome kids who do not speak proper English into the boardroom? Towards the end of my talk, a few began to understand my message. If they gave the students the information they need to survive in the real world and offered them more options for success, maybe then they would become better students. And maybe if they knew they could become financially successful even with a low paying job they wouldn't be so tempted by the high paying profits from drugs, sex, and crime.

3. Keeping score builds self-esteem, When I returned to my 25th high school reunion, I ran into Susan who had been the class brain. While we were in high school, Susan was a straight A student as well as member of student body government. Although she was not voted most likely to succeed, many people felt she should have been. After high school, she went to a prestigious small woman's college and again excelled in

academics.

At our 25th reunion, she was still the charming and friendly person she had always been. Yet I could sense something was troubling her. After the pleasant re-introductions, she began to open up and tell me about life after college. She had returned to Hawaii with her new husband and soon had a job with a large island company as a vice-president in charge of something. Things were going along fine until her husband announced he was leaving her for another woman co-worker and moving back to Virginia. At the age of 35 she became a single mom with three children to raise on her own. At the same time, the company she worked for announced a down-sizing and she was laid off. She immediately went back to school for her Masters degree and took a job with one of the largest banks in the state, working her way back up the ladder but at a much lower pay scale. Her ex-husband then asked that he be allowed to reduce his child support payments because he had started another family. After she finished bringing me up to date, all she could say was "This is not the way I thought my life would end up after school."

All through school she was a happy, high self-esteem person. She had great grades and immense popularity. Yet as she later said, "In the real world, good grades don't mean that much. Today at age 49, I have nothing to keep score with except a lower salary, higher taxes, greater expenses, college to pay for, not much set aside for retirement, and no social life. Few men want an instant family."

After the reunion, my wife and I sat and talked about life and happiness. In the discussion, my conversation with Susan came up. I said to my wife, "All through high school, Susan was a very happy, self confident person. Everyone knew she was smart, had great grades, and would have no problem being accepted to the best schools in the country."

My wife Kim sat for awhile and asked, "What do you think happened?"

I thought for a moment and said, "I think she failed to find another grading system."

"Why do you say that?" asked Kim.

"Because in school, she had great grades. But after school, her score card looks a bit tattered. And while I was in high school, I was the one with the bad grades. And although I had poor grades, my self-confidence was high because my rich dad had given me a different score card to guide my life. A score card that would count in school and out of school."

"You mean your financial statement?" Kim said with a smirk and a hint of sarcasm.

I nodded my head.

"So are you saying that everyone should be

graded financially?" Kim asked with a smile. Knowing me better than anyone else in the world, Kim was ready for a not too normal answer.

"No," I said. "I think everyone should have a score card that keeps their self-esteem high. I'm not saying it has to be a financial scorecard. It could be a score card on how many times they hug their kids or how many hours they spent with their kids. The most important thing is that once school is over, a person should find a scoring system that keeps their self-esteem and self-confidence high. Because what is life without self-confidence?"

"And your score card is your financial statement." Kim added.

"That's correct." I replied. "A financial statement is like a report card. It reflects back at you how you're doing in the world of money. If I don't like the grade then I know I need to make some changes. Susan, who does not have an accurate grading system, does not really know where she is financially, and is not able to make life corrections. She is doing what she was taught to do. When she lost her job, she goes back to school and looks for another high paying job. The problem is, with the Internet and growing global competition the idea of a high paying job for life may get harder and harder for her to find as she gets older. Employers today want young workers who will work for less, work harder, and think faster. Today, many of the technical skills taught in schools are obsolete in less than 18 months. How can she work harder and compete for those high paying jobs?"

"I think she is afraid to look," said Kim softly. "I'll bet she takes life one day at a time...just like that old TV show."

"You're probably correct." I replied. "With the divorce rate so high, many young people unintentionally become single parents with kids to support. I'll bet that it is tough to think about the differences between earned, passive, and portfolio income, when the main thing they think about is survival."

Kim smirked again. "So to you a financial statement is a report card. And what about people who don't like their report card?"

"Well, if they were properly educated in school, they could look at their grades and make corrections early in life. But as we speak today, there will soon be millions of people in the Western World who will come to the end of their working days and find out they have a failing grade in personal finance. There are millions of our generation, the Baby Boomers, who do not have enough set aside for retirement. Who will take care of them when their retirement savings run out? Who will take care of them when they are unable to work? Who is going to pay for the huge medical bills senior citizens incur? Their kids?" The government?"

"So you think that young people should be taught to use a report card they can use for life?"

I nodded my head. "Instead of teachers grading students. Teach the students to be financially literate and grade themselves financially as well as teach them how to make corrections financially. Then we might have a more financially responsible society instead of a society that thinks the government should solve our financial problems. How can the government do that? It can barely solve it's own financial problems. The government should receive a failing grade on their report card for the way they manage their own Income Statements and Balance Sheets."

Kim just smiled and nodded her head. She had heard this lesson many times.

A Note from Ann Nevin, Ph.D.

Both financial and word literacy are learned by children and adults in much the same way. The biggest differences between children and adult learners is that adults often must 'unlearn' (or at least 'set aside') their previous ideas and that is why children often learn faster!

The way that children learn in school often results in children deciding that learning is not very much fun. This is sometimes an outcome of the type of feedback that they receive: "No, you're wrong." "You are making too many mistakes." "You earned a D on that assignment." "You are a poor student."

When children play a game, however, the feedback comes from the process of playing. They make the corrections naturally, or their peers guide them to take corrective action. Very rarely will another child say, during a game of 'Monopoly' or chess for example, "You earned a D on that move!"

The most powerful feedback is the kind of feedback that leads to self discovery about the type of corrective action needed to take to get different results. When the child hears a question that encourages him or her to think about how new actions will lead to new results, then the child feels encouraged and will try again. With this type of instructional feedback children often begin to self-correct!

Receiving praise and compliments for the aspects of performance only inspires the child to try again. In addition to feedback that leads to corrective action, praise for specific actions can achieve a powerful effect. When you show your appreciation and excitement each time you notice the children discovering a new distinction or becoming more skilled in manipulating the exchanges involved in CASHFLOW for Kids, you build the children's self esteem. You've heard the saying "You can catch more flies with honey than with vinegar." The power of celebrating with positive reinforcement (appreciation, praise, encouragement, smiles, and applause) results in happier and more confident children who are more eager to learn on their own.

A Note from Sharon Lechter:

In accounting, financial literacy begins with understanding the Income Statement and Balance Sheet. Unfortunately, many people leave school barely able to keep their checkbook in order.

In all three of our CASHFLOW Games, the score card is not the game board but the players' Financial Statements. By playing any of the games, you and your children are improving your financial literacy while having fun. Each game has a different level of sophistication and focuses on different financial topics. Yet the score card or report card remains the player's financial statement.

The financial statement is also the report card in the financial world. All too often, I have come across adults who have been failing financially for years never knowing how badly or deeply in debt they were getting. How could they since they had no way to measuring their financial life's progress? Learning is easy if you start young and learn a little at a time. Learning is tough when you're over 40 and find out you not only have to correct a lot financially, but you also have to learn a lot about financial education. Correcting is easy if you have a basic financial education. Correcting is difficult if you have to go back to grade one and begin with the basics of financial literacy. So please use this educational game and book to teach your children while they are young.

A report card is not for reward or punishment. It is simply a tool meant to measure one's progress. A financial statement tells you if you are on the right financial track or the wrong track. It lets you know when you're doing well and when you need to make corrections. A person's financial statement is a measure of a person's financial IQ. That is why financial literacy is important. If you cannot read financial statements, you will not know how to measure your financial IQ. I encourage all parents to teach their children about the Income Statement and the Balance Sheet. Let them know that it is the financial report card of life.

CHAPTER 6
Building Block #5

Seek The Truth From The Facts

I begin this chapter with the "your house is not an asset" story described earlier. It best illustrates the concept of fact versus opinion.

In my home, my dad always said, "Our house is an asset and our biggest investment."

In my rich dad's home he always said, "Your home is not an asset and if it is your biggest investment, you're in financial trouble."

Being a young boy, I really did not know whom to believe. I wanted to believe both dads yet the contradiction greatly disturbed me. One day, I brought the subject up with my real dad by saying, "Mike's dad says our home is not an asset."

"Oh don't be silly," my dad said. "Everyone knows a house is an asset."

"But why does he say it isn't?"

That question seemed to be one of those questions a child asks an adult, the answer to which the adult really does not know and does not really want to take the time to explain.

"I don't know why he says that." My dad replied. "Why don't you ask him."

"I did," I replied. "He said it was because with our home, the money flows out of our pockets, not into our pockets."

"Well that might be the way he defines an asset, but if you ask any banker they will tell you that our home is an asset." Now I was even more confused because my dad had his banker to back him up.

The following weekend, after working in rich dad's store, I repeated to my rich dad what my dad had said. Since it was one of our regular Saturday afternoon class sessions, my rich dad said, "That is a good point. Let's make that question the lesson of the day." With that he picked up the phone and called his banker. And although it was Saturday, his banker agreed to come over. Remember those were the days of smaller banks and more personalized service. Plus, my rich dad was one of his largest customers.

"He'll be over shortly," Rich dad said. "But before he comes over, I'm going to teach you a very important lesson."

Mike and I sat there while he collected his thoughts. We knew that when he was about to say something important he usually paused for awhile, shuffled with papers on his desk not really looking for anything in particular, and then the words of wisdom would come forth. Finally he said, "If you want to be successful in life, you must know the difference between facts and opinions."

Then came another period of silence.

"That's it?" I asked. "Is that all there is to this important lesson?"

Rich dad nodded his head in silence.

The room was quiet and still for a very long two minutes. He said nothing more and Mike and I just sat there, two young boys in front of his desk, our feet swinging under the wooden chairs, waiting for the thunderclap.

Finally it dawned on us that his silence was reinforcing the importance of his simple statement. When it had sunk in that he had imparted a very important bit of wisdom, Mike finally said, "So what is the big deal? What is the big deal about knowing the difference between facts and opinions?"

"Everything," said rich dad quietly. "Everything."

And then again there was silence.

Finally after another long minute, he spoke again. "Most people's financial lives are messed up because they make decisions based upon opinions rather than facts. The worst thing about that is they then fail to know the difference between an opinion and a fact."

"What is the difference?" I asked.

"Good question," said rich dad. "A fact is something that you can prove by seeing, touching, or feeling. An opinion is something not verifiable at the moment."

"Give me an example," Mike asked.

"OK," said rich dad. "I have a dollar in my pocket. Opinion or fact?"

"Who cares?" I said tiring of the exercise.

"Because you have to care if you want to be successful," said rich dad. "Because this simple example is the basis of today's lesson. It has to do with why your dad thinks his house is an asset and I don't. It's one of the main reasons the rich have more money."

"Just because you take the time to know if something is a fact and if something is an opinion?" I asked.

"That's correct," said rich dad. "This is a very important lesson in the world of business, investing, and money. One is not right or wrong. A fact is not better than an opinion. Just know the difference. Now, back to my question of the dollar in my pocket." Rich dad then restated the question. "I have a dollar in my pocket. Fact or opinion?"

"Well, you might have a dollar in your pocket," Mike said. "But until I see it, what you're saying is an opinion."

"And could it be a fact to me but an opinion to you?"

"Yes," I replied. "If you have a dollar in your pocket then it's a fact to you."

"Good," smiled rich dad. "It could be a fact to me, but until I show you the dollar, it will always be an opinion to you."

"So do you have a dollar in your pocket?" asked Mike. "I assume you do since you always have money."

"You'll never know," said rich dad. "I'm not going to tell you just so that you will always remember this lesson. This lesson about knowing the difference between facts and opinions. It is a very important distinction."

About that time my rich dad's banker walked in.

"Ed," my rich dad said. "You're just in time. Thank you for coming over to help me teach a financial lesson to these two young future customers of yours."

Are You Lying or Telling the Truth?

"OK, Ed," Rich dad began. "When you say that a person's house is an asset, are you lying or telling the truth?"

"Oh not that question again." Ed said shaking his head. "Your dad and I go around and around on this point all the time."

"So what is the answer?" asked rich dad.

"I'm telling you the truth." Ed said a little defensively. "It's just that you look at things a little differently than we were trained to look at things."

"Just give these boys the facts," smiled rich dad seeming to enjoy his friend squirm a little. "Just the facts."

"OK," said Ed. "I'll show you the facts and why your dad asks me such tough questions." Ed took a breath, gathered his thoughts and said, "The facts are, when you buy a house through our bank, the mortgage document we both sign shows up in your liability column. That is why he says your dad's house is a liability."

"Good," smiled rich dad. Rich dad then took out a pencil and drew the following diagram for Mike and me to see.

Your Balance Sheet

Assets	Liabilities
	Mortgage

After finishing his sketch, he looked up and said, "Go on. Tell these boys where that mortgage shows up on your balance sheet."

Ed the banker squirmed and shook his head with a grin, "You're a tough man."

"Tell them. Just tell them the facts," rich dad said gently.

Ed who was also my dad's banker smiled and said to me, "Your dad's mortgage shows up in the bank's asset column."

Rich dad then completed his drawing.

Bank's Balance Sheet

Assets	Liabilities
Your Mortgage	

"What?" I blurted out looking at the diagram. "When you say our home is an asset, you're not really telling us whose asset it is. You mean our home is really the bank's asset?"

"Well, if you look at it from Mike's dad's point of view, that is how he sees it. But from your dad's point of view he sees it as an asset. And it is in many ways," Ed said defensively.

Rich dad laughed and said, "Just stick to the facts." At that point, rich dad reached for his yellow legal tablet and drew the following diagram.

Your Financial Statement

Income Statement

Income

Expense
Interest

Balance Sheet

Assets	Liabilities
	Mortgage

The Bank's Financial Statement

Income Statement

Income
Interest

Expense

Balance Sheet

Assets	Liabilities
Your Mortgage	

"These simple diagrams are the facts. Aren't they?" asked rich dad as he finished his sketching.

The banker nodded his head. "Those are the facts. Your mortgage shows up in your liability column and in our asset column."

"You see boys," said rich dad. "When they call this a balance sheet, what most people do not know is that a balance sheet cannot balance on one person's sheet. It must balance on at least two person's sheet."

"I'm really confused," I said.

"Most people are," said rich dad. "Just remember this. For there to be an asset, there must be a liability. For there to be income, there must be expense. But both transactions cannot occur on only one financial statement. There must be at least two. I call it double entry accounting. But there must be at least two different financial statements." Rich dad then drew the following diagram.

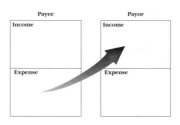

"This is a more complete financial picture," said rich dad. "Things must balance. So for you to have an expense, then it must be someone else's income. It has to balance."

"You mean that it takes at least two financial statements to make sense. That for every one of our family's expenses, that expense is someone else's income. And for every debt we have listed in the liability column, that same debt is someone else's asset? Is that why you're saying that it takes at least two financial statements to make sense?"

Rich dad nodded his head. "Now you're becoming much more financially literate. And once you understand that, you can begin to see which direction the cash is flowing."

"That is why you say by noticing which way the cash flows, you know the difference between assets and liabilities. The cash flow is the fact." I said quietly. "The cash flows from my dad's pocket into the bank's pocket. That is the fact."

Rich dad nodded his head. "And that is why I say seek the truth from facts. Too many people simply take the word of someone they think is an authority and accept an opinion as a fact. Just think of the long-term consequences of that little misunderstanding. That is why so many people all over the world struggle financially. They do not know the difference between an asset and a liability so they buy liabilities they think are assets. If they simply bought assets before they bought liabilities they would get richer and richer. But instead they buy liabilities they think are assets, and then they struggle financially and work harder and harder."

"But what about the value of the house?" asked Mike as he took the legal tablet and drew the following diagram.

Income Statement

Income
Expense

Balance Sheet

Assets	Liabilities
$50,000	$40,000

"What do you say when someone buys a house for $50,000, with $10,000 down as the down payment and a $40,000 mortgage. What about the $50,000 value of the house in the asset column?"

"Good question," said rich dad. "So what is the $50,000 in the asset column? Is it a fact or an opinion?

"Well, it could mean someone paid $50,000 for the property," I added.

"Yes," said rich dad. "But is that what it is worth today?"

"I don't know," I said. "It could be more and it could be less."

"Very good," said rich dad. "So until you sell the house, its value is an opinion. If you sell the house for more than $50,000, and the sale puts more money in your pocket than what it cost you, then and only then do you know it's real value and whether or not it was an asset or a liability."

"So this whole lesson is only about knowing the difference between facts and opinions," Mike summarized.

"That is correct," said rich dad.

"You're not telling them not to buy a house. Are you?" asked the banker.

"No," said rich dad. "All I'm doing is educating these boys into calling a spade a spade. All I am saying is don't buy a liability and believe it's an asset.

"Are you saying that Ed is lying to people?" I asked.

"No," said rich dad. "Ed is a banker. He knows the difference between an asset and liability and so should you. Isn't that correct Ed?"

"That is correct," said Ed. "We lend you money as long as you can afford to pay us back. We'll lend you money on a house to live in or a house to rent out for additional income. We'll lend you money on a car to use personally or on a car to be used as a taxi. It's your choice to borrow money for assets or liabilities. But we at the bank always know which side of the balance sheet your loans are. Your loans are found in our asset column and in your liability column. So if you go simply by the facts, your dad here is correct. We know the difference between an asset and a liability; facts and opinions. And in the banking business, we hear a lot of opinions, especially from people who are trying to borrow money. However, we must lend money based on facts. That is why we look at a person's financial statements before lending them money. We're not in the business to tell you what to buy. We don't tell you to buy assets or liabilities. If you want to go deeply into debt buying junk, that is up to you. It's your money. You can do with it as you please. All we want to know is whether or not you can pay us back. And the financial numbers, not the person, tell us that story. So your dad is correct. The rich borrow money to buy assets and the middle class borrow money to buy liabilities. But either way to us, they're assets."

Rich dad was rocking back in his chair, twirling his pencil between the fingers of both hands. He was grinning, seeming to know that Mike and I had just learned a very important life lesson. And it was. That one lesson has kept me very aware of the duality of financial statements, assets and liabilities, and the difference between facts and opinions.

Ed the banker stood and said, "Well, time for me to go. Is that what you wanted me for?

"One more thing," said rich dad. "Show these boys how their savings are being recorded at your bank."

Sitting down again, Ed took hold of the legal tablet and drew the following diagram.

Your financial statement

Income Statement

Income

Expense

Balance Sheet

Assets	Liabilities
Your Savings	

The bank's financial statement

Income Statement

Income

Expense

Balance Sheet

Assets	Liabilities
	Your Savings

"You mean you consider my savings a liability to your bank?" I asked.

Ed the banker nodded his head hesitantly. "The reason is because we have to pay you money for your money. Your money causes our cash to flow out of our expense column and into your income column. That is why your savings are your asset but our liability. Or as Mike's dad says, your savings cause money to flow out of our pocket so it's a liability. And since the interest we pay you flows into your pocket, then your savings are an asset."

At an early age, I was receiving one of the most important lessons in financial literacy. I could now see why my rich dad was so adamant about reading numbers, watching which way the cash flowed, and gaining the whole story for myself, rather than listening to other people's opinions. I realized that my highly educated but poor dad was literally blinded by his lack of financial literacy. Years later, when I pointed out to him that his mortgage was listed under his liability column, he still refused to believe that his house was a liability. His old opinions had blinded him to the facts.

"Now can I go?" asked Ed.

"No," said rich dad. "Just one more thing."

"And what is that?"

"Tell these young men the tax consequences between interest payments from debt and interest income from savings."

Ed the banker laughed, "Do you think they will understand it?" he asked.

"Maybe not fully today, but they will in the future," smiled rich dad.

Ed turned to Mike and me and said, "The U.S. Government gives you a tax break for being in debt. In other words, the tax code allows you to write off certain interest payments against your income."

"Does that mean that the government gives me

an incentive to be in debt?" Mike asked.

Ed nodded his head. "That is a way of looking at it. And the government taxes your interest income from savings."

"In other words the government punishes me for saving money," I said.

Ed nodded his head.

"Why?" I said.

Ed looked at Mike and me and said, "Boys, when you get older and richer you will find out why. As you get older just do as your dad here is teaching you. Learn the truth by following the trail of money."

Rich Dad jumped in, "OK Ed, so is Robert's dad's house here really the asset the bank wants?"

"What do you mean?" said Ed.

"What really is the asset you look at when you loan someone money to buy the house of their dreams?"

"Oh I understand," said Ed. Turning to the two boys Ed gathered his thoughts. "What your dad is getting at is that the house is not really the asset. In true financial terms, the house is collateral. Your dad is really the asset."

"My dad is the asset?" I gasped. "Not our house?"

Ed the banker nodded his head. "Your house is the thing of value that we take and resell if your dad does not pay the mortgage. That is why the house is called "collateral." And the mortgage is the called the "security." It is the agreement or what you boys call the I.O.U. The difference is our I.O.U. is secured by the house, the thing of value."

"But the asset is really my dad?"

"Yes and no," said Ed hesitantly. "Your dad is asking me to give you two years of business school in two hours. So it's a little more complex than a simple yes or no."

"But let's stick to the facts," said rich dad. "If a poor person, a person without a job and no income wanted to buy Robert's house, would you lend that person money to buy the house?"

"No," said Ed. "In most instances, if a person has no job we would not lend money on that house."

"Good," said rich dad with a grin. "But could a person without a job buy the warehouse I want to buy? Even though the warehouse costs over a million dollars."

Ed the banker hesitated for awhile. "Technically the answer is "Yes." Ed said reluctantly. "But again we are not comparing apples with apples."

"That is what I wanted to hear," said rich dad. "Tell these boys why it's not a case of apples to apples."

The banker glared at rich dad. "Because when we evaluate loaning money on your dad's house, we look at your dad, his job, his income, and how well he pays his bills. But when we evaluate this warehouse, we don't only evaluate the person. We primarily evaluate the warehouse."

"Tell them why," said rich dad.

"Because the warehouse with the tenant in it is the asset. It makes a lot of money. Our risk is low. A house used as a personal residence does not make money," Ed replied. "So the person buying it is the asset. That is why a person without a job cannot buy the same house as a person with a job can buy. The reason is the person with the job is the asset. Not the house."

"Thank you," said rich dad. "I'll call you about the warehouse on Tuesday."

"We'll have the check ready," said Ed.

Our little classroom in rich dad's cramped office was silent. There was a lot of information that needed to settle into our young minds. "There is a lot more to understand," rich dad said finally breaking the silence.

Mike and I nodded our heads. There were many little distinctions we still did not understand and it would be years of further discovery for us to fully understand the power of the ideas we had just heard.

Finally I began to speak. "So my dad can only borrow so much if he is the asset?" I asked.

Rich dad nodded his head. "Your dad and much of the middle class borrow up to the limit of what their paycheck can afford. They borrow to what I call the "red line." And the red line is that point where income and expenses are the same. They get a raise and they rush out to borrow up to the new red line. That is why they don't get ahead. They borrow to buy liabilities they think are assets, never realizing that they are the asset. Not the things they are buying."

I sat there nodding my head. Slowly I began saying, "Because the banker wants the facts. And the fact is how much money you make and how much you have left to spend after your expenses are paid."

Rich dad nodded his head.

"And the banker will lend you a lot of money for the warehouse, much more money than you make because you are not the asset. The warehouse is the asset. It's the asset because it makes the money with or without you. Is that correct?"

Rich dad still nodding his head said, "You're beginning to make finer and finer distinctions."

"So you borrow money and get richer and my dad borrows money and gets poorer. Is that correct?"

"It's not correct, right or wrong," smiled rich dad. "In these instances those are the facts. When I buy that warehouse with money loaned to me from the bank, I will put more money in my pocket in a month than your dad earns in the same month. Your dad borrows money and he has to work harder and struggle to pay bills. Those are the facts. Your dad borrows money for a liability he thinks is an asset and I borrow money for an asset that is an asset. And I can prove it. It puts money in my pocket. I have the facts. Just ask Ed the banker."

"So there is good debt and there is bad debt," Mike said.

"It's not a matter of good or bad," said rich dad. "It's just a matter of borrowing for liabilities or borrowing for assets. The middle class borrows for liabilities it wants to believe are assets. That is the problem with not knowing the difference between facts and opinions. When it comes to money, the poor and middle class operate on too many opinions and not enough facts."

"So when you advise us to do our homework, this is an example," I said.

Rich dad nodded.

Continuing on I said, "The reason you can borrow more even though you earn less salary than my dad is because you borrow money for assets. He has more earned income but you have more passive income. Is that correct?"

"Good distinction," smiled rich dad.

"And my dad can only borrow so much because he only earns so much. But if you find ten more warehouses or other businesses, you will get richer and richer and work less and less. Just because you borrow to buy assets and my dad works hard and borrows to buy liabilities," I said as the lesson was settling into my brain.

"Even better distinction," noted rich dad. It's a very subtle distinction but the difference is a life of tremendous wealth versus a life of hard work and financial struggle. That is why the rich get richer. They know the difference between facts and opinions, assets and liabilities, and they borrow money to buy assets."

"But my dad couldn't go out and buy a warehouse today, could he?" I asked.

"I wouldn't recommend it," said rich dad. "But he could learn how to do it."

"What do you mean learn how to do it?" I asked.

"Remember the 4 green houses in 'Monopoly'?"

rich dad asked. You want to start small because you don't want to risk too much money. Understand that you will probably make a few mistakes. Losing money is part of the learning process. If you lose money it means you don't know something. So if you take losing money as a good sign that you are going to learn something you do not know, then the price of your education was small. If your dad went out and started with a multi-million dollar warehouse without first having bought the four green houses, that same mistake could be financial suicide."

"So you think losing money is good." I said.

"Yes," rich dad said emphatically. "As long as the price is small and you are humble enough to learn the lesson from the mistake. If you think the mistake was just a mistake and your arrogance doesn't allow you to learn from it, then the next time the price of that same mistake will go up. Mistakes are valuable learning tools. Don't waste them because in the world of business, the mistakes get more expensive each time you make them. Learn from the mistake the first time and the lesson will be cheap. Don't learn from it and the price of the lesson goes up."

"So my dad could buy that warehouse if he started with the small green houses first," I stated.

"He can do whatever he likes," rich dad replied. "I would recommend he start with the small green houses. But what often happens is people often say, "I'll invest when I have a large chunk of money. And when they do, that large chunk is soon gone. That is why I say do your homework. Start with small green houses and work your way up. But most people want to make the big killing in the market and that is what happens. Their fortune gets slaughtered."

"Is it because they don't know the difference between facts and opinions?" Mike asked.

"And much more. They lack experience and education. Most people are financially illiterate. They take advice from the wrong people. The list goes on. That is why I say get financially literate. Start with small green houses and learn how financial statements work. If you can read the numbers you can pick up small problems in the numbers before they become big problems. If you can read numbers you can pinpoint what is working and what is not working."

"Real estate sounds like a business," I said.

"It is a business," said rich dad. "That little green house is a business. The dirt under the house is really the real estate. The person who rents it from you is your customer. The banker is your money partner. That is why I recommend you start with building businesses and buying real estate. Not only are you converting earned income into passive income, you are gaining powerful financial education and experience while you're young. As you get older and begin building bigger businesses and buying bigger pieces of real estate, your education and experience will be awesome. You will be earning more, working less, and paying less in taxes. That is financial intelligence."

"So why start with building a business. Why not go straight to real estate?" I asked.

"Because it's easier to buy real estate if you have lots of money and experience. People are more willing to deal with you if you have money and they tend to avoid you if you're broke. I still need to have $200,000 to buy that warehouse. Could I buy it for no money down? Of course, but it is easier to buy it if you have money and it also makes better sense from the risk point of view. If you build a business, you have a better chance of being a better businessperson. If you're a bad businessperson, you won't have money anyway. So if you're good, you will have the cash flow to buy all the real estate or stocks and bonds you want. Always remember that your business buys your assets. You don't."

"But can't a person who doesn't have a business buy real estate?" Mike asked.

"Sure," said rich dad. "Anything is possible. But if they don't have that source of income or cash, it takes much longer. That is why I recommend they build a profitable business first. A business has more tax advantages than someone who works for money, which means you can acquire more real estate faster. Ask any banker and they will tell you that there is nothing more profitable than a well-run small business. Once you learn to run a small business machine, and if the cash flow is strong, your accountant will recommend you buy real estate because the accountant wants you to convert earned income into passive income to help shelter your other income from taxes."

"And what if someone doesn't want to do any of those things you mentioned?" I asked.

"Then that is why we live in a free country. We all have that choice of being rich, poor or middle class. That is a choice only the individual can make," said rich dad.

"Does everyone have the potential to be rich?" I asked.

"I would like to think that everyone has the potential," rich dad replied. "But not everyone has the desire."

"Is that a fact or opinion?" Mike asked.

"It's my opinion," smiled rich dad.

Distinctions

1. Most things have the potential to be assets or liabilities. For example, a house could be an asset or a liability. My rich dad's warehouse could be a liability if the tenant moved out and no one moved in. Education can be an asset if the information is accurate and useful and it can be a liability if the information is obsolete, inaccurate, or misleading. Intelligence is not about how smart you are but about making finer distinctions.

2. Facts are not better than opinions, yet problems arise when opinions are used as facts. For example, people get in trouble financially when a salesperson says, "The value of this house will go up." Whenever someone says that to me, I simply say, "Will you guarantee that, put it in writing, and pay me if it doesn't go up?" That usually ends

that opinion.

A few examples of opinions that can lead to problems in one's life (financial or otherwise) are:

1. "You should marry him. He'll make a good husband."
2. "Buy this stock. The price will go up."
3. "Go ahead ask her out. Her boyfriend won't mind."
4. "The best way to avoid taxes is to buy a bigger house."
5. "She's an honest salesperson. She wouldn't steer me wrong."
6. "You'll never be rich."
7. "He is smarter than you."
8. "The price of real estate always goes up."

As I said, most of our problems or troubles in our lives begin when we take opinions and use them as facts. Opinions such as "You should find a safe, secure job, buy a big house, and invest for the long term." I am not saying that this is bad advice. All I am saying is that is exactly what it is. It's advice. And most advice is opinion, not fact. Many times all people need to do to clear up problems in their lives is first find the opinion they used as a fact...the opinion that got them into all the trouble in the first place.

3. Seek the Truth from Facts. Learning to be financially literate makes it easier to find the truth from the facts, or as rich dad always advised, "Seek the truth from the facts." One of the reasons I recommend you teach your child to be financially literate is because they will be better able to seek the truth from the numbers. For example:

A. An asset will put money in your pocket. When you look at the financial statement, the facts will tell you the truth. (An audited statement is best.) Using as an example my rich dad's warehouse, this is what the banker would see.

Income Statement

Income
Rent From Warehouse
Expense

Balance Sheet

Assets	Liabilities
Warehouse	

B. A liability will take money from your pocket. Using my dad's house as an example, this is what my rich dad would see.

Income Statement

Income
Expense
Mortgage Payment

Balance Sheet

Assets	Liabilities
	Dad's House

In this case, the facts are that money is going out. There is an expense but no income. So for that moment in time, my dad's house was a liability because it was taking money from his pocket. It was the fact that it took money from his pocket that put it in the liability category. Now if my dad had rented the house out and it put money in my dad's income column, then the house would have been an asset, at that moment of time.

The transaction would have looked like this.

Income Statement

Income
Rental Income From Dad's House

Expense

Balance Sheet

Assets	Liabilities
Dad's House	

So the distinction my rich dad made was based on the direction of the cash flow.

This is why bankers and other sophisticated financial professionals analyze a financial statement. They first look at the income and expense column to determine what are assets and liabilities. They make their decisions based on the facts. The masses go on popular opinion, simply calling their home an asset and putting it under the Asset Column in their mind...and never checking the facts. They make financial decisions based upon opinions and not the facts. And as I said, most problems are caused by opinions used as facts. To raise your child's financial intelligence, teach them the difference between facts and opinions.

NOTE: I am often asked, "If I pay off my mortgage, will that make my house an asset?" I would answer with a question, "Which way is the cash flowing?" In the case of most personal residences, a house is still a liability, even without a mortgage. Without a mortgage it would be a smaller liability. The reason it is a liability is because there are still expenses related to owning a house. If you look closer, looking for finer distinctions, your financial statement will look like this even if you do not have a mortgage.

Income Statement

Income
Expense
Property Taxes On Your House
Repairs On The House
Electricity
Water
etc.

Balance Sheet

Assets	Liabilities
	Your Houe without A Mortgage

So at that moment in time the house would remain a liability even without a mortgage. Now if this person took in a renter for their basement let's say, and the rent was $100 more than those expenses, then that house would swing over to the asset column. It would be an asset simply because it was putting money into your pocket of the income column of your financial statement.

> C. Appreciation costs money. I often have people argue with me saying that, "But my house has gone up in value."

This is an opinion

The *fact* is that they must include the carrying costs of owning that home as just described (property taxes, repairs, etc.) before determining any gain from the increased value of their house.

If rich dad was buying a $100,000 house to live in he knew he would have to sell it for at least $200,000 in 7 years to get back his original purchase price and all of the carrying costs (assuming a 7½% interest rate).

While you could argue that owning a house is better than renting, it is still an *opinion*.

Rich dad would point out that if you knew for certain the value of that $100,000 house would go up, you should buy five of them. Live in one (a liability) and rent the other four (assets). This way the cash flow from the four would more than pay for the carrying costs of the one you live in. He would end by asking, "are you so sure the market value will go up or is it your *opinion?*

Note from Ann Nevin, Ph.D.

Critical thinking skills are one of the most important learning outcomes that educators and educational psychologists applaud. But the sad truth is that most high school students graduate without being able to use their critical thinking skills to help them live their adult lives. A major reason for this dismal outcome seems to be that critical thinking is not taught in ways that are meaningful or relevant or interesting to our children. All too often in schools, children are required to accept opinions as facts, without verification. We require students to repeat back answers we give them instead of asking them to do research and find their own answers based on facts and opinions. Too often in school we require children to conform rather than question the answers they are being required to accept as the truth.

Because this book and CASHFLOW for KIDS, use a variety of methods through stories, analogies, metaphors, and the process of playing the game to show key Financial IQ concepts and principles, children are able to develop critical thinking skills!

Although CASHFLOW For KIDS is simple, it does prepare your child to move on to CASHFLOW 101 and to make finer distinctions. Education is a process. It is a process of making finer distinctions. And the finer the distinctions we can make, the more our intelligence increases.

A Note from Sharon Lechter CPA

I often see people in great financial difficulty simply because they use opinions rather than financial facts to make decisions. I do not know where they get their opinions from but often those opinions lead them to financial failure. Professional advice is often powerless against their opinions.

As an accountant, I strongly recommend you teach your children to learn to keep accurate financial records. If they start young it will become a habit. All too often I meet adults without a clue on their financial position in life. They attempt to make important financial decisions based upon opinions of where they are financially. Financial insanity is caused by financial opinions used as facts.

Please take the time to use this game as a teaching tool, and as you play the game with your children, please educate them about the following important distinctions.

1. Know the difference between fact and opinion. Your mortgage on your house is a fact, a definite amount. The value of your house is an opinion. While the game does not deal with this specific issue, the players can quickly learn that their own home does not generate income but does cost their family money each month through payments on the mortgage.

2. As your child plays the game, the players will begin to learn that there are two parties to every transaction, the individual making the payment and the one receiving the payment. Discuss with the children that for every liability you have, there is a corresponding asset on someone else's balance sheet.

3. The Advanced Rules of the game add variation to both the cost of assets and their related

incomes. Not only do these rules demonstrate the effects of volatility in the marketplace, but also the impact of opinion vs. fact when valuing assets.

4. The concepts being taught from this book and the game are sophisticated concepts that most adults do not know. So please take your time and be patient in teaching these concepts along with the game. A child's mind can become overloaded just as an adult's mind often is. So play the game often and take your time reinforcing these concepts. It is repetition that will reinforce the principals taught through financial literacy.

CHAPTER 7
Building Block #6

Money Grows Like a Tree

My poor dad often said, "Money doesn't grow on trees."

My rich dad often said, "Money does grow like a tree."

In one home, there was never enough money. No matter how much money my dad made we were always short of cash. In my rich dad's home there was too much money.

I was at a lecture listening to a child psychologist a few years ago, and she was talking about how a child between the ages of 5 and 14 often develops what she called "The Winning Formula." Her research had discovered that during that time a child often makes decisions that create the formula the child follows for the rest of his or her life. She said that a child needs to feel that the winning formula he or she has adopted is OK with the parent, regardless if the parent agrees with the child's winning formula or not. For example, if the child states that he or she wants to be a movie star, the child needs to feel the parent's support of that winning formula for life... even if it is not the formula the parent wants for the child. She said rebellion or arguments begin if the parent counters or dismisses the child's wishes. Such as saying, "Go to school," "Get a job," "Stop dreaming about being a movie star." "Arguments," she said "are often clashes between one winning formula and another."

She went on to say that five things happen at this stage of mental and emotional development.

One, the child is encouraged to follow his or her own formula. The child feels secure in knowing that the parents will love them no matter what they do.

Two, the child gives in to the parent's wishes, suppressing his or her own formula and adopts the parent's formula. For example, a child may give up the idea of pursing a career in Hollywood and become a doctor instead...simply because everyone else wanted a doctor in the family.

Three, the child realizes that he or she cannot live up to his or her own dreams much less the dreams and aspirations of their parents. If this happens, the child may develop a defeated, "What's the use?" type of attitude. The child may want to become a doctor but believes he or she lacks the academic potential to make it through medical school. If this attitude is strong, the child may also believe that no matter what he or she does, he or she will never that great at anything. This child may give up on his or her winning formula and become aimless and begin to drift.

Four, the child may simply rebel against parents wanting to impose their formula upon the child's formula.

And five, the child may feel that the parent doesn't care at all and the child may adopt a formula that will get the parents attention, in one way or another.

Some children may adopt a formula to excel and thus gain their parent's attention. For example, the child may become the academic star or become a great athlete to gain the parent's attention. Or a child who is not getting the attention wanted may adopt a formula that would get attention by shocking the parent. In other words, a formula that seeks to get even and to hurt the parent for their neglect, even though the parent may care deeply.

As she spoke, I found my mind drifting back to my own childhood. Memories began to reappear from the past. I remember at the ages of six and eight being extremely poor. The fear of not having enough money permeated the entire family. Out of six people in the family, five had been in the hospital at one time or another. The only one who was not sick was my dad. I could vividly recall my dad sitting at the tiny kitchen table doing his best to figure out how he was going to pay all the medical bills and still have enough money to feed the family. Being the oldest of the four children I remembered feeling helpless and not knowing how to give my dad a hand. I remember wishing that I knew how to make a lot of money so I could help my dad and our family out.

When I was eight our family moved from Honolulu to the Big Island of Hawaii so my father could take a better paying job. Moving meant he had to put his education on hold. While in Honolulu, he had been working on his advanced degree. However, the cost of having a family, plus the added burden of medical bills put an end to his studying. He took both a job and a part-time job to make ends meet. But the situation did not change. Even after the medical bills were paid, the fear of not having enough money ran through the entire family like an electric current. Although he made more money, our family was always short of money. At the end of every month, my mom and dad often argued saying things such as, "Where did all the money go? All I do is work, and no matter how much money I make, we never have any money left over." One night, while my dad was away at a PTA (Parent, Teachers Association) meeting, I came across my mom crying in the kitchen. When I asked her what was wrong, she showed me a sheet of paper with the bank's logo at the top. The bank statement was a goldenrod color. This being the days before high-speed computers, the entries were typed in with a manual typewriter. About two thirds of the entries were typed in with black ribbon. The bottom one third of the numbers were typed with red ribbon. When I compared the current bank statement with the previous month's statements, it was easy to see that more numbers were typed in red each month. At the age of eight, I clearly understood what "Being in the red." meant. All I could do was hug my mom at that moment. But deep down inside I felt helpless.

"Your dad gets very angry every time I show him our bank statements," my mom said. "He gets angry and blames me for spending too much money. Son, I don't spend too much money. Most of the money goes out before I have anything to spend. So I write checks and the bank sends us these over-draft statements in red."

"What does Dad do?" I asked my mom. "What is he doing to solve this problem?"

My mom looked up at me and said, "All he says is that he'll work harder. But I say what difference does it make? Even if you work harder, you still make the same amount of money. Then he gets angry."

I did not know how to solve our family's problem at that moment, but I made a silent vow that I would find out. The following year, our family moved across town, I changed schools, and I met Mike and his dad...the man who would become my rich dad.

With these vivid pictorial memories playing in my head, I could hear the psychologist saying, "A boy needs to feel very secure with his relationship with his dad during these years. If a boy feels that his dad disapproves of the boy's winning formula, then the relationship begins to break down. The boy may go in search of another father figure. The child may seek a new parent or mentor to guide them. Boys and their mothers often have a strong bond simply because a mother often loves the child regardless of what the child does. In other words, mothers show their love differently than fathers. But if the relationship between father and son is strained, the father and son may begin to fight, mentally, emotionally, and physically. As strange as it may seem to women, this fighting is a way men sometimes express their love."

Sitting at home that night after the psychologist's talk, I realized that while much of what she said did not apply to my life personally, there were things she said that were right on target. Here I was, nearly 48 years of age, and there were certain memories that were as clear as if they were yesterday. That evening, I distinctly recall making the decision to seek the answers to the mystery of money. I was nine years old. I remember distinctly deciding to follow closely and listen to my rich dad. I really did not know what he knew or if he knew what I wanted to know, yet something inside of me was attracted to him. He seemed to have the answers I wanted. My real dad seemed very preoccupied with his career, his title, and his own importance to the community. Far more than he seemed to be concerned with the financial well-being of his family. Recalling the memory of my mom softly crying over bank statements printed in red had caused a split between my dad and me. I knew I had to find the answers my dad did not have.

2 Kinds of Money Problems

"There are two kinds of money problems." My rich dad said to me. "One problem is not having enough money and the other problem is having too much money. Which problem do you want?"

As stated previously in Rich Dad Poor Dad, one dad taught me how to write resumes and the other taught me how to write business plans. My rich dad was constantly writing or updating his business and investing plans. "Have you heard that saying, 'Failing to plan is planning to fail'?" he asked Mike and me one Saturday. Mike and I nodded our heads. "Well it's true." He said. "Most people have a plan on how to make their money but they do not have a plan on what do with their money after they make it. Those are the people who have problems related to not having enough money. If you have a good plan for your money before you make it, then your problem will be having too much money."

My poor dad's plan, or winning formula, as the psychologist called it, was a simple plan. His plan was to go to school, get a job, and work hard. He went to school to learn to make money but he never sought education to what to do with his money after he made it. It became obvious that his plan was to make money and buy a bigger house or a new car with each pay raise. That is why we as a family were always short of money long after the medical bills had been paid.

My rich dad's plan was to simply take earned income from the business he built, buy assets not liabilities, and have those assets generate passive income and portfolio income. In my rich dad's family, there was always a problem of having too much money. How do I know that? I know because my rich dad showed me his bank statements as well as his financial statements. I know because he took me to meetings with his bankers, lawyers, and accountants. I know because his accountant was always telling him that he had to take a bigger salary or donate more money. I know because my rich dad was constantly out looking for more investments to buy with his money. Soon, it became a full-time job for him. His earned income needed to be converted to passive and portfolio income rapidly. He was soon living on 30% of his gross income and invested the remaining 70%, which only made his problem of having too much money grow. He had so much money coming in that he spent most of his time looking for more investments, which in turn, put more and more money into his pocket. By the time he was fifty, he had to hire one person just to manage his income from investments and another person to give money away to charities.

Recently, I read that Bill Gates, the founder of Microsoft, also has the same problem. Not only does he have people earning money for him full time, he has people working full-time to invest his money and to give his money away. In just one of his charitable trusts, he is required to give away $325 million each year. He and my rich dad had the same problem.

A Lasting Impression

The single most important impression my rich dad made upon me relative to money was this idea that there could be too much money. Having been raised in a family where having not enough money was a deep emotional trauma, just the idea that I could attain a life of having too much money was a beacon in the darkness.

In my real family, there was a deep emotional fear of not having money just to survive. That emotional fear tainted our thoughts and outlook on life. My poor dad often said, "Do you think money grows on trees? "Do you how hard I work to put food on the table and to clothe you kids?"

The fear of not having enough money ran our family. That fear affected our way of thinking, often paralyzing us, and it eventually became our family's reality. We feared not having enough money so much that we never had enough money in real life. The fear and thoughts of a shortage of money became a self-fulfilling prophecy. As stated in the Old Testament, a passage goes, "And the word became flesh and dwelt amongst us." The fear of not enough money had become flesh in our family.

My rich dad often consoled me. "I show you my bank statements and investment portfolio to let you know that there is plenty of money in the world. Your mom and dad show you bank statements that teach you that there is not enough money in the world. You must always remember that both worlds are possible. Your job is to choose the world you want for your life." The picture of both types of bank statements has stayed with me all my life. I know that if not for my rich dad I would have followed in my parents' footsteps, down a path of hard work, large bills, and a chronic fear of not having enough money. Instead I followed in my rich dad's footsteps. A world of financial intelligence, a healthy respect for the power of money, and the knowledge that I could determine what kind of world I wanted to live in. Even though I had no money at that time, I chose a plan that would lead me to a life of too much money.

Distinctions

1. There are three worlds of money. The world of the rich, the poor, and the middle class. One of the advantages the children of the rich have is that they come from a world of plenty. That environment of abundance of money affects their outlook and view upon the world. As stated earlier rich children are often first introduced to investments, trust funds, businesses, accountants, lawyers, bankers, at an early age. Their priority is often first investing, and second career. In poor and middle class families the priority is often first career, and then owning a big home and a nice car. Then they may think about investing. The difference I have noticed is that by having investing as priority one, the children are introduced to the idea of having more than enough money, of

being good stewards of their money, and of being mindful of putting money aside for the future.

By playing CASHFLOW for KIDS with your children, you begin to teach your children to budget…to teach them to create abundance from what they have, regardless of how much they may start with. My family had the bad habit of buying a bigger liability each time we got a few extra dollars, like a new car or bigger house. My rich dad taught his son and me to take 30% of our gross income and put 10% into a piggy bank for savings, 10% for investing, and 10% for tithing (charity or church donations). By teaching us to take 30% off the top right away, he was teaching us to budget from abundance. By taking 30% right off the top, we were teaching ourselves that there was plenty of money, rather than not enough money to buy what we wanted. He often said, "Rich people pay themselves first. They take 30% for themselves right away. Then they spend money and pay bills. Poor people and middle class people spend first, and then try to save with what is left…but the problem is, there is seldom anything left."

He drew this diagram:

Rich people	Other people
1. Earn	1. Earn
2. Tithe	2. Spend
3. Invest	3. Tithe
4. Save	4. Save if anything is left
5. Spend	

He would then draw a line from the "Other people" to the "Rich people" and say, "These people always work for these people."

2. The power of three piggy banks. As a child, I had three piggy banks. As an adult, I still have three piggy banks. Although I do not use the three piggy banks like I used to, they still serve as a simple reminder to me that there does exist a world of too much money. And that is a world determined by me. If I cannot control my desire to spend money, then my piggy banks will be empty and I will live in a world of not enough money. If I can develop the habit of paying myself first, then I know I will live in a world of too much money.

When people ask me what they can do to straighten out their financial situation, I tell them to buy three piggy banks and begin to put money, even if it is only a dollar a day, away in each bank, everyday. Most do not take me seriously and look for more sophisticated answers. Yet I am serious. I recommend this therapy because by doing this simple exercise everyday the individual is reprogramming their mind from a world of not enough money to a world of an abundance of money. If not established as a habit, the chances are the person will revert back to a world of scarcity and not enough money.

3. Increase the percentages. I often hear moans from my adult audiences when I say take 30% right off the top. The reason they moan is because they are currently living on 110% of what they are making and to live on 70% of their gross would be painful and a dramatic change in lifestyle. To those people I say, "Then start with 3%, but most importantly, start. Start by putting 1% of your gross into each of the three piggy banks. So if you make $1000 a month gross, before taxes, put $10 a month in each piggy bank. I still hear moans. That is why I say start your kids young so they don't have to go through the pain of financial withdrawals.

After you start with 30% as part of your plan, work to continue increasing that percentage. In other words, instead of 30%, work to save, tithe and invest 40%, then 50%. When I read the biographies of the ultra rich, most of them invest at least 50% of their gross income. In other words, they invest 50% and live on 50%. It's that habit that makes them rich. I was listening to Sir John Templeton of the Templeton Funds and he said that even when he and his wife were struggling financially, they still had the habit of investing a minimum of 50% of their gross income. That habit transferred to how he managed his family of funds may be why his funds are so successful.

Poor people live on 100% and work hard the next month only to live on 100% again. As stated earlier, my rich dad eventually got to where he was living on 10% of his gross income and reinvesting the rest. So if you want to become very rich, begin with a small percentage going to saving, tithing, and investing, and have a plan to increase it. My poor dad always said, "I'll begin to invest when I have some money left over." The problem was, there was never any money left over because in his mind, there was never enough money anyway.

4. Don't live within your means. My poor dad worked hard and tried desperately to live within his means. He often said, "Don't spend money. We need to live within our means. My rich dad always said, "Don't live within your means. Learn to expand your means." By expanding your means he meant focus on increasing your income rather than trying to live within your income. He also said, "The poor try to live within their

means. The middle class try to extend their means by borrowing. And the rich increase their means by planning, budgeting, building businesses, and investing wisely."

Today, I hear financial advisors saying to people, "Cut up your credit cards." While that is good advice, the reality is you don't necessarily get rich by cutting up your credit cards. I also hear them say, "Live within your means." That too is good advice but it alone will not make you rich. Generally such advice is good advice for the poor and middle class. But if you want to get rich you need to learn ways to expand your income...and that is what CASHFLOW for KIDS is teaching your children while having fun. The game demonstrates the power of building a strong asset column and how it results in increased cash flow.

When I say to people that my rich dad lived on 10% of his gross income, most people say, "I couldn't do that. That's not enough money." Most say that because they fail to ask how much 10% of his gross was. Rich dad was a man who started with very little, yet his habits allowed him to keep seeing a world of more and more money. He did not live below his means. He increased his means by simply putting more and more money into his asset column. He built businesses and invested in real estate. For him money did not grow on trees, but it did grow like a tree as his empire kept spreading out.

My highly educated but poor dad continued to attempt to live within his means. The only problem was that as he got older, his means continued to decrease while inflation continued to increase. As I said he always saw a world of not enough money and that world became true for him. My rich dad saw a world of plenty of money and that world became true for him.

5. Our educational system teaches scarcity. The Western World has adopted the economic theory of economist Thomas Malthus. When you read current books on economics, the premise of Western economics is that "Economics is the study of the allocation of scarce resources."

This economic theory is old and obsolete. It was an economic theory popularized at the start of the Industrial Age. Thomas Malthus was not an economist but a Protestant minister. The reality today, in the Information Age, is that via the alchemy of technology we can produce more and more from less and less. With modern technology, even the so-called scarce resource of gold can today be found in mines that we thought were mined out. We can find oil where we thought there was none. And in the world of machinery, just look at computers. In the early days of computers, they were large, took up lots of space, required many people to run them, and were exceedingly expensive. Today, we have computers costing less than a $1,000, which are tiny, and can do much, much, more than the larger computers of old.

Problems arise when people still think in terms of Malthusian economics. Today I still hear people say, "I deserve a raise because I've been at this job for five years now." That is an Industrial Age idea. In today's world of cheaper technology and greater global competition, to make more money each of us needs to produce more to be paid the same wage we were paid yesterday. The good news is that inexpensive technology allows more of us to do just that. Today, it has never been easier to do more with so much less. That is the good news. The bad news begins when people subscribe to the obsolete economic theory of scarcity, and think they should be paid more for doing less.

There are two books written by Paul Zane Pilzer, a person I call the "Information Age Economist." His books are "Unlimited Wealth" and "God Wants You To Be Rich." I recommend both books for people who are ready to drop old economic theory and move on to more contemporary and, in my opinion, accurate economic theory.

6. Attitude is everything. Recently I was talking to a young man in Dayton, Ohio. During our talk he said something I have heard many times. While discussing with him the path to becoming rich he said, "I once delivered a television set to one of the richest men in this town. I was surprised to find him sitting in his big house all alone. I then realized that most rich people are rich because they have stepped on so many people's feet, that no one wants to be around them."

After his statement, I asked him why he remembered that one picture of wealth. After thinking for awhile, he finally said, "That was the first time I had ever been in a rich person's house and that is what I remembered."

The point of this distinction is that we all tend to see what we want to see. All too often, I meet people who are not well off financially, and they have some opinion about rich people that puts the rich in a light that is less than kind. For example I have heard people say such statements as,

1. "I don't want to be rich because the rich aren't happy."

2. "The rich are snobs and greedy."
3. "Rich people don't care about poor people."

Psychologists call such broad negative generalizations and character assassinations, a "denigration of character." Which means a person needs to put someone else down to make himself or herself feel better. In my family, my mom and dad justified their lack of financial wealth by saying that they were more highly educated than my rich dad and that they were concerned about helping people rather than exploiting people as they thought my rich did. They did not like my rich dad because he had hundreds of employees and they thought he did not pay them enough. That is why they said he exploited them. They saw the world from the "E" quadrant and my rich dad saw the world from the "B" quadrant.

In summary, it is in our homes that a child's winning formula for life begins to take shape. It is my opinion that a child be given as much choice to choose a winning formula that can best support their lives in the short term and in the long term. It is a family's attitude that best gives that child the freedom to choose.

When it comes to the subject of money, a question to ask yourself is, is your home a place of abundance or a home of financial scarcity? As you play the game CASHFLOW for KIDS with your children, I suggest you begin to talk of a world of plenty rather than a world of scarcity. That is one of the most important lessons a child can learn, as they begin to form their winning formula.

A Note from Ann Nevin, Ph. D.

I want to emphasize the importance of teaching children to have a positive mental attitude for problem solving. When children learn at an early age that what they think matters (such as deciding in the game CASHFLOW for Kids whether or not to buy 'that doodad'). Or that when they do a certain action there are specific consequences they control (such as when they invest their money, their money earns money), they learn that they can influence their lives. This results in the child having what is called "an inner place of control." Adults with an inner place of control are more likely to be happy in their selected life careers, more likely to be healthy, make more money, and are more likely to take responsibility for what happens to them compared to those adults without an inner place of control. Choosing to change the way one thinks about a concept (such as deciding not to choose the scarcity model of economics) requires a powerful inner place of control.

Another important educational psychology concept in this chapter is the importance of reprogramming the mind by choosing to change the thoughts we think. When this happens, the mind also begins to "see" what had not been seen before. By increasing your distinctions about learning styles and knowing how you learn best, you can decide to "study smarter" instead of "study harder."

Similarly, instead of deciding to "work harder" (putting more and more effort into a work situation that isn't getting the results you want), you can "work smarter" by increasing distinctions about economics, finance, and cash flow. This book and the game CASHFLOW for KIDS teaches such distinctions and can assist you in raising your children's financial IQ.

A Note from Sharon Lechter CPA

Having studied literally thousands of financial statements of individuals and corporations, I can honestly say that a financial statement is really a reflection of the core beliefs of the person or the company. In other words, people afraid that there is not enough money manage their money from that frame of reference. People terrified of losing money manage their money differently than people who come from a winning point of view on money. I have also noticed that there are charitable poor people and charitable rich people. On the other side, there are also many stingy poor people and stingy rich people. Reading financial statements as a profession is an interesting way of seeing into a person's financial core.

CASHFLOW for KIDS was created to teach your children that there is a world of financial abundance if they manage their money well. The game rewards behavior that promotes financial wealth and steers children away from behavior that causes financial scarcity. As a CPA and a mom, I am happy to be associated with a product that reinforces the idea that each of us has the power to control our financial destiny. Each of us has the power to determine that destiny by knowing what to do with money once we receive it. With each dollar your children receive, they have control over their financial future. That is why we want children to learn not simply to be rich, but more importantly that they ultimately have the power to determine their financial destiny. Their financial future is their choice and no one else's.

CASHFLOW for KIDS was created to support you as you teach your children about money and family finances. Children start learning how to manage money and finances at a very early age by watching and listening to their parents. Often the parents' habits around money management are learned by their children.

Always remember that the best way to reinforce the financial education learned through the game is to be aware of how you as adults talk about money at home. Is your home a home of abundance, or a home of scarcity? Do you say "Money does not grow on trees." or do you teach your children that "Money grows like a tree." With care, love, and proper nourishment, money does grow like a tree. With a little care and patience, you can teach your children to grow oak trees for their future.

CHAPTER 8
Building Block #7

Watch What You Say

When people ask me what was the most important difference between my rich dad and my poor dad, I say without hesitation, "It was their choice of words."

As a little child, I began to notice that the words my dads used were reflected back to them in the lives they led.

Hence when I am asked, "How do I start to begin to become wealthy?" I always say, "Begin by watching your words. Words may be free, yet they are the most powerful tools you posses."

My dad had a habit of saying things such as,

1. "I can't afford it."
2. "You can't do that."
3. "The reason I'm not rich is because I

have you kids."

4. "I'm a school teacher and school teachers don't earn much money. That is why I'm not rich."

On the other hand, my rich dad instructed his son and me to choose our words carefully. He used to say, "Watch what you say. Rich people speak with rich words and poor people speak with poor words."

A few years ago, I was speaking to a small group of people who lived in an economically depressed area of San Diego, California. The mixed group of people was concerned about their children. Like parents everywhere they wanted the best for their children. During the meeting a young mother stood up and said, "You were fortunate enough to have a rich dad. We don't have that. We don't have much money. What can we do to give our children a financial head start in life?" Without hesitation my response was, "Begin by changing the words you use."

The young mother remained standing looking at me. "Are you saying my English is not good?" she said a little defensively. "Are you saying I don't speak proper English."

"No." I said cautiously. "Your English is excellent. When I say that you may need to change the words you use, I mean to learn and use more words of commerce around your home and if possible, in your schools.

"Please give us an example of these English words of commerce," said one of the women sitting in the room.

"OK," I said thinking for awhile. Looking the mixed group of people I said, "My company will go public in a few months with an I.P.O. In the meantime we will need to secure some mezzanine financing and offer some preferred shares of stock with subordinated debentures. After the I.P.O. we may raise more capital with a secondary offering."

I looked around the room and then asked, "How many people understood what I just said?" Out of the 45 or so people sitting in the room only 2 raised their hands. I thanked them for their honesty and said, "The reality is, very few people understand what I just said."

"And those are the English words of commerce?" asked one person.

"Those were just a few of them," I replied. "In reality, there are many, many more such words of commerce. And each word means something unique and important."

"And the more a person understands those words, the easier it is for them to acquire great wealth," said a young man sitting in the front row.

"That is correct," I replied. "You see, although we all speak English, we really do not speak the same words. And if we do not speak the same words, then we tend not to understand each other."

"But that is true for anything," said one of the young men in the group. "If I like cars and another guy doesn't, we don't hang out together."

"You're getting it," I said. "So your children can leave school with excellent grades but know nothing about the language of the rich, which is the language of commerce."

"You mean rich kids learn those words at home?" asked one of the women.

"Some do. They learn it simply because their parents often use those words." I said.

"Do you mean to say that we send our kids to school but they fail to learn the language of the rich?" asked another mother incredulously.

I nodded my head slowly. "What I am really saying is this. If you want to elevate the financial well-being of your group and your people, you first need to start with introducing new words. Words that schools do not teach you. That is where the process begins."

If I said, 'Non-collateralized funding vehicle.' How many of you would know what I was talking about?"

This time no one raised his or her hand.

With a smile, I then said, " How many of you understand what a credit card is."

With a roar of laughter, almost everyone raised their hands, even some of the young children.

Laughing I said, " A non-collateralized funding vehicle and a credit card mean almost the same thing."

"You mean one description used the language of commerce and the other word was the language of the people to describe the same thing?" asked the young man in the front row.

I nodded my head. "When we go to elementary school and high school, we learn the language of academics. We learn the language that school teachers use. If we go on to Law School, then we begin to learn the language of law. Doctors go to Medical School to learn the language of medicine, secretaries learn the language of secretaries and so on."

"So many of our young people do well in school but learn nothing about the language of the rich. Instead we learn the language of the middle class," said the young woman.

"And the values," I said quietly. "Which is why you hear so many people say, 'I'm looking for a safe, secure job. And then I'm going to buy the house of my dreams because a house is an asset.' They use those words because those are the words they are familiar with."

"And what did your rich dad teach you?"

"Instead of telling me to go look for a company to work for, he advised me to go out and build businesses."

"But not everyone can build a business." said a middle-aged man in a baseball cap from the back of the room. "Not everyone can be rich."

I stood there in silence letting the words echo in the room. As the seconds ticked by, the silence became chilling as the words continued to echo through the room.

"Change my words," said the same middle-aged man. "Why should I change my words? Look, I came here because I've been laid off twice. I have bills to pay, kids to feed, and the best advice you can give me is to change my words. I need a job that pays me a decent wage so I can support my family. I don't want to be rich. I just want enough money to live on and all you can say is change my words. You're full of it." With that he stood and stormed out of the room.

As he was leaving, three other people stood. One of the three, a woman about my age turned and said, "I've listened to rich con men like you most of my life and I'm not going to listen any longer. It's you rich people that exploit us honest hard working people. And then you stand there and say that your rich daddy told you to build businesses. Your rich daddy taught you the words of commerce. Well good for you. Well my daddy didn't. And because he didn't, I'll never be rich. And all you can say is watch my words. What a waste of time this is." She then turned and joined the group heading out the door.

I had to remind myself to take a deep breath as I stood there. My breathing had stopped. Still I said nothing. Although the outburst was unexpected, I thought it best to let the words echo in the minds of those that remained behind.

Finally the young woman with the baby stood and said, "So that is what you mean by watch your words," she said.

I nodded my head.

"That is what you mean by our words reflect back on to us in the lives we lead," said the same young woman.

Again, I nodded my head.

"I don't want my baby growing up around people who speak like that," she said.

Another woman stood and said, "Well I did grow up in a home where we said things just like that. Those people who left could have been my parents. Good hard working people who struggled financially all their lives."

"And how did that affect your life?" I asked.

"Well, I sure didn't learn much about money. I learned about anger and frustration about money," she said. "I learned that the way out of poverty was to go to school so I could get a good job...and that is what I did. But I must admit that I still feel the same frustration about money my parents did. Sometimes I get very angry when I hear people like you speak about making a million dollars in a year and I fight hard to keep a $45,000 a year job."

Another woman stood and said, "You know the hard part is that I have those thoughts screaming in my brain too. When it comes to money, my mind just won't shut up. My mind has all the same angry and frustrated thoughts about money. I just don't say it out loud like those people who left did. What can I do?"

"I'm glad you said that," said a man about my age. "I have those same thoughts too. And for years I've gone to motivational seminars to learn to think positively. To say nice things and be kind to others. And I do, and it works. But I still feel the same frustration about money, bills, dreams, and the desire to get ahead. I really want to provide a better life for my family. But positive thinking and positive speaking only go so far. They don't pay the bills."

After thanking them for staying, I drew a deep breath, collected my thoughts and began to say possibility the most important lesson I know about money. "How many of you have read the book, 'Think and Grow Rich' by Napoleon Hill?"

About 5 of the 40 or so remaining raised their hands.

"And how many of you have read 'As A Man Thinketh', by James Allen?"

This time only 1 out of the group had read the book.

"If you notice both books place emphasis on the word think. The word 'think' is a verb just as the word 'work' is a verb. And a verb is an action word. And when it comes to money, the people with the biggest money problems work hard for money and fail to change their thinking about money. They work instead of think. As I often say, Napoleon Hill's book is titled, Think and Grow Rich, not Work Hard and Grow Rich."

After a moment of silence, the young woman with the baby stood and slowly began by saying, "So we do what we think."

I nodded my head.

"So to change what we do we first need to change what we think."

I nodded my head again encouraging her to continue on.

"And what we are doing is what we are thinking. And what we have been thinking is go to school, get a good job, buy a house, buy a car, spend money on the good life and work harder to pay the bills."

I stood silently waiting for her to continue on.

"And I won't get rich thinking that way. All I'll do is work hard and pay bills. Then I get angry and frustrated because I'm not rich and guys like you are making millions of dollars."

The room waited as she gathered her thoughts.

"And all I am doing is what the words in my head are telling me to do. And if I don't change my words I will keep doing the same thing." She said staring with a glazed look. She had a glazed look because she was now doing as my rich dad often said, "Watch what you say." And she was staring out with a glazed expression because she was watching what she has been saying silently to herself for most of her life, on the inside.

The room was very quiet as she stood there alone watching what she had been saying to herself. I suspect the rest of the room was doing the same thing. It was one of those moments of deep quiet and introspection. It's a moment when we take a break from the chatter of the world and a silence sets in, inside our minds and in our souls. It is moments like these that lives have the greatest possibility of changing. It is in these moments when our minds stop chattering for awhile, and inspects the winning formula that we adopted years ago. It is in these moments of silence, we may decide to make some changes in our formula. It is at these moments that we hold the power to change our life's destiny.

"So I work hard, buy a nice house, pay bills, enjoy life, have kids, and live for today because that is what I decided I wanted to do." The young mother said. "And my life won't change until I change the formula. Until I change the cassette tape in my head."

"They don't have to be big changes," I said. "Just change or add a few words. You see I like all the same things you do. I think most of us want the same things. It's just that a few words are missing."

There was an older man sitting in the back of the room. He had been sitting quietly listening to the dialogue in the room. As he stood he said, "Whenever I needed more money, I simply went out and worked harder. I would go and get a part-time job or work some overtime for the boss. And what you are saying is that those are the words of a working-class man."

"Well I didn't say it quite in that way," I replied softly.

"No, no," he said. "I understand. You've not been making working-class people wrong. I just want to understand that what you are saying is that I use working-class words and you use a rich man's words in your mind. You use the words of commerce and I use the words of labor. Is that what you're saying?"

"Yes," I said. "That is what I am saying."

I could see that he was a well-groomed gentleman as he stood looking back at me.

I asked him, "What do you do for a living?"

"I'm an engineer for the city," he said. "My salary is good but with kids ready to go to college, all I'm doing is working extra jobs trying to save money for their education. The problem is, I have less and less time with my children, something I want more and more of. They'll be gone in a few years and all I've done is work instead of spending quality time with them. On top of that, I'm telling them to do the same thing I'm doing."

I thanked him as he took his seat and then I said, "Positive thinking is important because attitude is very important. But attitude without a change in personal vocabulary does not change much. If you want to be rich, I recommend using the words of the rich. Unfortunately, too many people use the words of commerce without knowing the definition of the word, and that gets them into even more trouble."

With that comment questions came flying out of the audience, "What do you mean we use words but don't know the definition of them?" asked one of the young women. "Give us an example."

"Well, what does the word mortgage mean?" I asked.

There was a moment of silence. Finally the same young woman asked, "Doesn't it mean debt?"

I nodded my head. "That is what it means in many ways, but it's strict definition comes from the French word 'Mortir' which is the French word for death. So the word mortgage literally translated means 'Engagement until death'. And in many ways, that is what is happening to millions and millions of people. They spend their lives working hard, paying bills, engaged in debt until death. These are the same people who use the word asset when they should be using the word liability. That is what happens when you use a word that you do not know the definition of. The power of the word still has power."

"Any other words we should know about?"

asked a member of the group.

"Well, real estate is an interesting word." I said. "Most people think real estate means real, something you can see, touch, or feel. Or as they say, 'It's for real.' Or that it's a tangible asset instead of being a paper asset such as stocks, bonds, and mutual funds. But the real definition comes from the Spanish word for royal. In other words, real estate really means an estate that belongs to royalty. And today, it still belongs to royalty."

"Why do you say it still belongs to the royalty?" asked one person. "Don't you own it after you pay off the mortgage?"

"It seems that way." I said. "But if you make a very fine distinction, and look at your financial statements, you will see that even if you pay off the mortgage, the property will always have a property tax to be paid. In other words, even if you think you own it, you still have to pay for it. Saying it more bluntly, the property still belongs to the royals who still control the government. If you think your property belongs to you, just stop paying that property tax and you will soon find out who really owns your real estate, with or without a mortgage."

"OK," said one of the men. "We can give our children a better future by teaching our young people the words of commerce. You really think that will help?"

"It would be a good start." I said. "Just look at the former Soviet Union. Everyone wonders why Russia has had a difficult time switching from

Communism to a Capitalist system. But how can they change if their people and their educational systems do not know or teach the language of commerce? How can a free market economy exist when people still think that government should take care of them? How can they be rich if they do not know the language of the rich? How can people become rich when they have been trained to look for job security instead of look for investment opportunities? How can they become rich if their own words say "Look for a job" instead of "How many jobs can I create?"

The young mother stood up. "The reason giving poor people money doesn't work is because the poor don't know what do with the money. Is that what you're saying?"

I nodded my head.

"So we work hard for money and you have money and people work hard for you. Is that what you're saying?"

This time I grit my teeth and back up a little as I nod my head. Her energy level had gone up. It seemed that she had made some finer distinctions and some new lights had gone on in her mind.

"So if we begin to teach our children the words of the rich, or the words of commerce, we begin to raise the financial well-being of our entire community. You're saying that economic change must begin with education. Is that what you're saying?"

"Yes." I said. "That is exactly what I am saying. There are approximately 2 million words in the English language and our lives are limited to those few words we use. Most people use fewer than 5 thousand words on a regular basis. There are plenty of words to choose from so help yourself. But remember to choose your next words carefully. Change begins with changing our words. For those of you who have thoughts that you don't want in your head, all you have to say is "I don't choose to have these thoughts." You have a right to choose what you want to think. And if those thoughts persist, simply ignore them. But always remember what my rich dad's advice. He said, "You cannot always control what you think but you can control what you say. If you do not want to think something, simply don't say it. If you persist with that practice, those unwanted thoughts will eventually fade away. They will have less and less power over your life. So choose and speak only the words you want. Maintain a positive yet realistic attitude and begin speaking the words of commerce, the words of wealth, the words of the rich. Because words affect our thoughts and our thoughts affect our actions and our actions affect our lives and our futures. And the good news is that words are free."

Distinctions

1. Today it is easier than ever before to gain access to the words of commerce. In school, I was not a very good reader and in real life, while I read constantly I still find my reading skills lacking. As I said in the beginning of this book, to survive in school and to raise my IQ I had to find a way of learning that

best suited me.

Over the years I have found that I learn best by active seminars, by having mentors who have done what I want to do, or by reading and listening to audio tapes. The Information Age, through the magic of audio tapes has made the great mentors of the world available to virtually everyone. Your bookstores are filled with audio tapes created by great people of commerce, wealth, and success. The best thing about audio cassettes is that I actually hear the person speaking in their own voice, with their own inflections, and tones. It's like being right there with them. And even better, I simply push the rewind button and I can listen to them over and over again, without asking them to repeat what they said to me. In the Industrial Age, you had to go sit at the foot of the master. In the Information Age, the master can sit with you wherever you want to sit.

I have noticed that people who fail to improve their vocabulary also fail to improve their lives. Instead of progressing they stagnate. Just like their IQ, instead of increasing with age, they fall behind with age. That is why I am a firm believer in repetitive and continuous learning. As a regular habit, I read books and if I like the books I will look for a tape from that individual. I will listen to the tape over and over again because I want to add to, as well as improve, the words I have stored in my brain. Going along with my rich dad's advice of "Watch what you say." the other side of it is "Watch what you listen to."

A Note from Ann Nevin, Ph.D.

For education to be effective, that is to take hold in the child's reality, there needs to be three things. They are:

1. Attitude
2. Subject, Word, Definition, or Object
3. Relevance

For example, Robert's rich dad had a very positive attitude towards the game of 'Monopoly'. And because he had a positive attitude, when rich dad showed Robert the little green houses, which are the object or subject, in this case, Robert paid attention because rich dad let him know that little green houses were important. The benefit that Robert had at a very young age was that his rich dad made the little green houses relevant, almost immediately. He did that by driving Robert and Mike to his real little green houses. In other words, the boys related 1. Rich dad's attitude towards the game of 'Monopoly' to 2. The little green houses and 3. Rich dad's real little green houses. At that moment the boys understood their rich dad's winning formula for financial success. On that day, that three step process became real. It became reality for those two young boys.

If Robert's rich dad had a negative attitude towards the game and to owning investment real estate, I suspect that too would have had a long lasting impact on his life. I have been told that Donald Trump's father was a real estate developer in New York and trained Donald in his business. Small wonder we see so many dazzling buildings in New York with the name Trump on them. So much of learning begins with attitude and attitude can go in many directions.

The problem that we educators face is that a child's attitude towards the subject we teach is often not an attitude that inspires learning. For example when I speak of the subject of mathematics, most people react with a pained attitude towards learning that subject. And then worst of all, most students really do not know how the subject of math relates to their real lives, especially higher math such as Calculus, Algebra, and Trigonometry. The reason Robert enjoyed reading his surfing and baseball magazines was because of the same three step process.

The beauty of CASHFLOW for KIDS is that it involves all of the child's learning modalities. The game requires reading, talking, moving, and critical reasoning. There is a lot of relevance in the game. The child learns a new word and immediately and physically relates it to the financial statement and the game board. The most important thing a parent can provide is attitude. Please be aware of the words you speak and the attitude from which those words come. For example, if you as the adult say, "Oh that is a stupid game." the child's attitude is affected. Or if you say "I don't like businesses, I like stocks." this too will affect the child's attitude towards the subject. And worst of all, if the child asks you to play the game and you say, "Not now dear, I'm too busy working. We've got bills to pay and I don't have time to play with you." I ask you to think and do as rich dad would advise, 'Watch what you say.' Especially around young children who love you, want your approval, want to please you, and often want to be just like you."

A Note from Sharon Lechter CPA

While I was a practicing accountant, I often felt that my clients and I were not from the same planet, much less speaking the same language. I'd say things like cut down on your debt, and they would run off and buy a new boat, telling me they had just bought an asset. Or they would work very hard and then wonder why the rich work less, earn more, and pay less in taxes. When I attempt to explain to them the distinctions between the three different types of income, they would stop listening. Instead of changing and opening their minds up to new ideas, most would go back to their old formula of work hard and complain about how hard they work and how much they pay the government in taxes. Some people say that ignorance is bliss. But in my professional opinion, financial ignorance is expensive in both time and money.

Words are very important. Words can bring us together if we speak the same words, and words can push us apart if we do not use the same words. I am thrilled with the financial and accounting words your children will learn and add to their vocabulary by playing CASHFLOW for KIDS. In my own family, playing the game has helped bring our family closer because we now have more financial words in common. Instead of being frustrated because we do not seem to communicate, we can now make finer distinctions and speak more precisely about the subject of money.

We at CASHFLOW Technologies, Inc. trust that this educational product will assist you in making your child's financial future a little brighter and a little more secure. My desire is to have this product enrich the lives of your children and their children to come. In the Information Age, financial literacy is vital for financial security. And financial literacy begins with understanding the words of commerce.

Thank you for your interest in your child's education.

Take Action

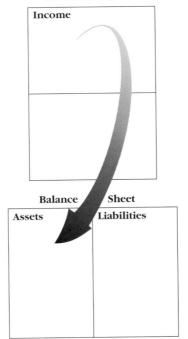

Income Statement

Income

Balance   Sheet

Assets | **Liabilities**

This is what CASHFLOW for KIDS wants to teach you children.

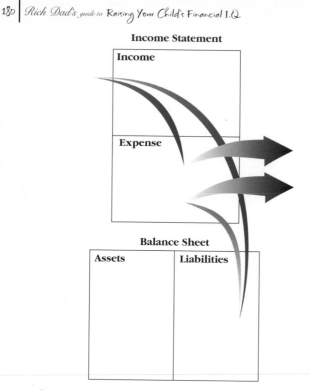

This is what others want to teach your children.

As my rich dad says, "If you don't teach your children about money, there are many people who will."

We at Cashflow Technologies create our educational products for you and your families in the hopes that this information will give you more choices in the future. We are entering an era of unprecedented financial opportunity as well as financial change. There will be market booms and market busts. While most of us would love to have a crystal ball so we could predict what to do financially in the future, I am afraid such a crystal ball doesn't exist. So in this era of great change, instead of trying to predict what will happen, I suggest we be prepared for whatever happens. Always remember what my rich dad said, "One of the reasons the rich stay rich is because they know how to do well when times are good and they tend to do even better when times are bad."

Thank you for caring about your education and your child's education. I trust this book, game, and audiotape have helped in preparing you and your children for the ups and downs of the future.

Robert Kiyosaki

About the Authors

Robert T. Kiyosaki

Robert Kiyosaki is the author of Rich Dad Poor Dad, an international best seller that focuses on what the rich teach their kids about money that the poor and middle class do not. He is also the creator of the financial board game CASHFLOW™ and other inventive financial products.

"The main reason people struggle financially is because they spent years in school but learned nothing about money. The result is, people learn to work for money… but never learn how to have money work for them." says Robert.

Born and raised in Hawaii, Robert is fourth-generation Japanese American. He comes from a prominent family of educators. His father was the head of education for the State of Hawaii. After high school, Robert was educated in New York and upon graduation, he joined the U. S. Marine Corps and went to Vietnam as an officer and a helicopter gunship pilot.

Returning from the war, Robert's business career began. In 1977 he founded a company that brought to the market the first nylon and Velcro "surfer" wallets, which grew into a multi-million dollar worldwide product. He and his products were featured in Runner's World, Gentleman's Quarterly, Success Magazine, Newsweek, and even Playboy.

In 1985, he co-founded, an international education company that operated in seven countries, teaching business and investing to tens of thousands of graduates.

Retiring at age 47, Robert does what he loves best… investing. Concerned about the growing gap between the "haves" and "have nots", Robert created the board game CASHFLOW, which teaches the game of money, here before only known by the rich. Robert was awarded a U.S. patent for this innovative educational game.

Although Robert's business is real estate and developing small cap companies, his true love and passion is teaching. He is a highly acclaimed speaker on financial education and economic trends. His life-changing work has inspired audiences from 50 to 35,000 throughout the world. Robert Kiyosaki's message is clear. "Take responsibility for your finances or take orders all your life. You're either a master of money or a slave to it."

During this time of great economic change, Robert's message is priceless.

Sharon L. Lechter, CPA

Sharon Lechter has dedicated her professional efforts to the field of education. She is a C.P.A., publishing executive, wife and mother of three.

Sharon graduated Summa Cum Laude with a degree in accounting from Florida State University. She went on to be one of the first women to join the ranks of what was then one of the big eight accounting firms, the CFO of a turn-around company in the computer industry, tax director for a national insurance company and founder and Associate Publisher of the first regional woman's magazine in Wisconsin, all the while maintaining her professional credentials as a CPA.

Her focus quickly changed to education as she watched her own three children grow. It was a struggle to get them to read. They would rather watch TV.

So she joined forces with the inventor of the first electronic "talking book" and helped expand the electronic book industry to the multi-million dollar international market it is today. She remains a pioneer in developing new technologies to bring the book back into children's lives.

"Our current educational system has not been able to keep pace with the global and techno-logical changes in the world today. We must teach our young people the skills, both scholastic and financial, that they will need not only to survive, but to flourish, in the world they face."

As co-author of both Rich Dad, Poor Dad and The CASHFLOW Quadrant she turns her attention to another failing of the educational system, the total omission of even the fundamentals of finance. Rich Dad Poor Dad and The CASHFLOW Quadrant are educational tools for anyone interested in bettering their own education and financial position.

Ann Nevin, Ph.D.

Ann Nevin is Professor of Curriculum and Instruction at Arizona State University West. She earned her Ph.D. in Educational Psychology at the University of Minnesota. For over 30 years, Ann has researched methods of improved education based on modern advances in psychology, and implemented them into her classes.

Ann spearheaded a program in which she created an educational curriculum taught via the internet to students throughout the U.S. as well as internationally.

Ann has four children and five grandchildren. She currently resides with her husband, Rolf, in Phoenix, Arizona.

CASHFLOW Technologies, Inc.

Robert Kiyosaki, Kim Kiyosaki and Sharon Lechter have joined forces as principals of CASHFLOW Technologies, Inc. to produce innovative financial education products.

The Company's mission statement reads:

"To elevate the financial well-being of humanity."

CASHFLOW Technologies, Inc. presents Robert's teaching through products such as Rich Dad Poor Dad, The CASHFLOW Quadrant and the patented game CASHFLOW (Patent Number 5,826,878). Additional products are available and under development for people searching for financial education to guide them on their path to financial freedom.

Financial Education for the *Information Age*

Most of us know that schools teach us nothing about money. This is why I wrote *Rich Dad Poor Dad*, *The CASHFLOW Quadrant*, and developed *CASHFLOW™ 101*, a revolutionary product built around a patented and fun educational board game. These and other products of *CASHFLOW* Technologies, Inc. are designed to give you and your family the same educational head start in finance my rich dad gave me.

In preparing for the Information Age, the rules on how to manage your money have changed. You can no longer blindly accept the idea that your job is secure, that your hard work will be rewarded, that your house is an asset and your largest investment and that buying mutual funds is safe. The Information Age will require you to have more information to do well and succeed. *Rich Dad Poor Dad*, *CASHFLOW 101*, and *The CASHFLOW Quadrant* were developed for individuals like you who recognize the need for new education. People who realize that the Industrial Age is over and the Information Age has begun.

Robert T. Kiyosaki

KIDS
Enter and WIN!

CASHFLOW® 101
The Game! What the rich teach their kids about money.

CASHFLOW 101 – *CASHFLOW 101* was created by Robert Kiyosaki to make available the same education his rich dad gave him. It's a complete learning system that includes instructional audio tapes and a video. *CASHFLOW 101* gives you and the ones you love a financial head start in life.

To Enter The *CASHFLOW* Drawing:
1) Please complete the statement below.
2) Be sure to include your name, address and contact details on the following page. Send your entry to the *CASHFLOW* office nearest you.

Complete the statement on the next page:
(25 words or less)

It's time to get out of the rat race!

CASHFLOW 101
The MBA Program
for families
(A \$195U.S. value)

I love CASHFLOW for KIDS because...

_____

_____

_____

_____

_____

_____

_____

_____

I am ____ years old.

It's time to get out of the rat race!

Please fill out the following form, completely and legibly.
Entry void if not legible.

Your Name:_____

Your Parent's Name: _____

Address:_____

_____

City:_____State:_____

Country: _____Postal Code:_____

Phone:_____Facsimile: _____

e-mail:_____

Age: _____ Occupation (Parent): _____

(Optional for parents)

Education Completed: ❏ High School ❏ Trade School
❏ University ❏ Graduate School

Personal Status: ❏ Single ❏ Married ❏ No. of Children_____

Comments about book - *Raising Your Child's Financial I.Q.*:

_____

_____

Drawings will be held quarterly in each of the cities listed below.
Please send your entry form to your nearest CASHFLOW office.

North America/South America/Europe/Africa:
CORPORATE HEADQUARTERS
CASHFLOW Technologies, Inc.
6611 N. 64th Place • Paradise Valley, Arizona 85253 • USA
(480) 998-6971 or (800) 308-3585 • Fax: (480) 348-1349
Visit our website: www.cashflowtech.com

Australia/New Zealand:
CASHFLOW Education Australia
PO Box 1126 • Crows Nest, NSW 1585 • Australia
1800 676-991 • Fax: 1800 676-992
Visit our website: www.cashfloweducation.com.au